THE
UNBIASED
ADVISOR

THE UNBIASED ADVISOR

108 Ways to Make More Money,
Achieve Financial Health,
and Avoid Costly Investment Mistakes

WARREN MACKENZIE

Collins

Published by Collins, an imprint of HarperCollins Publishers Ltd.

Originally published by Second Opinion Publishing under the title *A Second Opinion On Your Finances*: 2005
First Collins edition: 2007

HarperCollins books may be purchased for educational, business, or sales promotional use through our Special Markets Department.

HarperCollins Publishers Ltd
2 Bloor Street East, 20th Floor
Toronto, Ontario, Canada
M4W 1A8

www.harpercollins.ca

Library and Archives Canada Cataloguing in Publication

MacKenzie, Warren A., 1946–
The unbiased advisor : 101 ways to make more money, achieve financial health and avoid costly investment mistakes / Warren A. MacKenzie.

First published under title: A second opinion on your finances.
ISBN-13: 978-0-00-648126-3
ISBN-10: 0-00-648126-4

1. Finance, Personal. 2. Investments. I. Title.
HG179.M2525 2007   332.024'01   C2006-905839-3

RRD 9 8 7 6 5 4 3 2 1
Printed and bound in the United States

Design by Sharon Kish

About This Book

So much rides on your investment decisions: your quality of life, your family's security, your retirement, and the future of those you love. Yet you may have little perspective on how well you're doing financially. You may be worrying that you're taking too much risk with your investment decisions—or that you're taking too little. You wonder, "What's a reasonable rate of return in the market? Am I making any mistakes that could be compromising my retirement plans? Is my advisor doing what is in my best interests?"

Now you can get a second opinion on your finances from Warren MacKenzie, a former financial advisor who offers a wealth of experience, knowledge, and plain old common sense. *The Unbiased Advisor* will help you

- take action to reduce risk and improve returns.
- ask your financial advisor the right questions.
- determine whether your investment portfolio is efficiently designed to reach your goals.
- be sure that your portfolio has a reasonable level of diversification.
- design your portfolio for maximum income tax efficiency.
- work toward the retirement you want and deserve.

Contents

Part 4
Measuring and Monitoring Risk

Part 5
Controlling Risk

Part 6
Planning Your Investment Strategy

Part 7

Sticking to Your Investment Strategy

Part 8

Paying Less to the Taxman

Part 9

Paying Less in Management Fees

Part 10

Betting on the Tortoise, not the Hare

Part 11

Avoiding Common Financial Pitfalls

Part 12
Following the Path to Financial Happiness

Introduction

When it comes to our health, most of us do not make major decisions based on the advice of one doctor alone. We seek out a second opinion. But when it comes to our financial health, many of us do invest based on the advice of one broker or bank manager. We may have niggling worries or even grave doubts about the advice we're getting, but we just hang on, hoping for the best. Then there are those of us who bypass doctors altogether, taking our chances on "alternative therapies." We are the do-it-yourselfers. Some of us do an average or even brilliant job of investing, but most of us take big risks. We make our decisions based on gut instinct, blind hope, and what we happened to read in the paper just before the RRSP deadline.

This book will serve as a second opinion on the advice you are following, whether it comes from an advisor or from your own instincts and experience. It will show you how to "manage" your advisor—or yourself. Specifically, this book will assist you in understanding what you need to know to make sure you're getting to where you want to go financially. Here are some ways it may help you:

- by confirming that you are on the path to financial security, in keeping with your financial goals. This knowledge will allow you to sleep well at night and enjoy life to the fullest
- by helping you understand that following the right investing process is more important than finding the right investment products
- by showing you that some adjustments to your approach are necessary, arming you with the questions and facts you need for discussions with your advisor
- by coaching you to find a capable advisor, if you do not have one, or at the very least by guiding you in getting your affairs in order if you continue to go it alone

A TALE OF TWO SISTERS

To explain the benefits of financial planning, I like to tell the story of June, one of my clients. (Names and some details have been changed.)

June became a widow at the age of 66. She and her sister, Rita, who was also a widow and had recently retired, had promised themselves that when they stopped working, they would treat themselves to a once-in-a-lifetime cruise around the world.

June owned a small home in Stratford, Ontario. Her total pension income from all sources was about $15,000 per year, and she had roughly $200,000 in her RRSP. This is not a huge amount of capital, but June lived modestly. Her financial plan showed her that if she earned an average of 7.5% on her investments, she would never run out of money.

Because of the way her portfolio was diversified, she was confident of two things: first, that she would indeed earn an average of 7.5% per year, and second, that she was unlikely to suffer a large loss even if the stock market dropped precipitously. She also had confidence in her advisor and was not worried about whether or not her portfolio was appropriate for her.

Her sister, Rita, had been the beneficiary of a large insurance policy. As a result, she owned a nice home that was fully paid for, and had investments of more than $1 million. But she had no idea how much capital she really needed to maintain her lifestyle.

The sisters booked the cruise and June savoured every moment of the vacation. She enjoyed the sun, the smells, the exotic foods, the excursions on shore, the entertainment, and the new friends she was making. Every day was an adventure, and she packed in many experiences and memories. For years, she was able to brighten her days by thinking of the trip.

Rita, on the other hand, had a miserable time. She was constantly plagued with doubts about the wisdom of taking the trip. She didn't know how much money she needed to maintain her lifestyle. She didn't know what rate of return she needed to earn on her investments. And she had no idea whether her investment portfolio was too safe or too risky. Because she didn't know how much money she needed, she kept thinking that the money she was spending on the trip could mean having to do without in her old age. Every time she looked at the price tag for the cruise, she chastised herself. How could she have been so foolish as to spend so much on something that was not a necessity? When Rita remembered the trip, she felt nothing but pangs of regret.

The difference between these two sisters was that June had a financial plan and Rita did not. Though not as wealthy as her sister, June knew how much she could afford to spend, and she knew she was spending within her limits. She was confident that her portfolio was well diversified. She enjoyed financial security.

LIFE GOES BETTER WITH FINANCIAL SECURITY

There's no doubt about it: life goes better with financial security. When money worries are eliminated, you have more time and energy to enjoy the other good things that life has to offer.

In more than 20 years of helping people with their finances, I have seen far too many people who are unhappy and anxious about their financial situation. In some cases, this worry overshadows their lives, puts a strain on their relationships, and even affects their health. I have long been frustrated by this situation, because I know that almost everyone can be financially secure—and more easily than they imagine.

To be financially secure, you do not have to have an exceptionally good job, marry into money, or give up the best things in life. You need the desire to be financially secure, you need to set goals for yourself, and you need a plan. This book will help you come up with that plan and work with your advisor to reach your financial goals. You will then begin to enjoy the peace of mind that comes when financial concerns disappear.

AN INDEPENDENT ASSESSMENT

In this book, I offer you an independent assessment. I do not sell stocks, bonds, mutual funds, or swampland in Florida (or anywhere else, for that matter). I am not pushing to manage your investments. Although I have worked for many years "in-house" with major financial firms, I now work as a member of a consulting practice that offers advice on a fee basis.

My professional qualifications include a bachelor of education degree. I began my professional career as a schoolteacher in Halifax, Nova Scotia, where I taught grades 7, 8, and 9. Although I enjoyed teaching, I wanted another challenge, so I became a chartered accountant (CA) and worked in that field for a number of years. The teaching experience was good preparation for what I have done in my career—I believe that the most helpful financial planners are good teachers to their clients.

For 15 years, I worked as a CA in public practice, and during much of that time I collaborated with an income tax specialist. I remember being struck by the number of doctors who were nearing retirement age but who did not have enough savings to maintain their standard of living if they stopped working. These doctors had earned high incomes throughout their careers but had invested unwisely. I also observed that most owned worthless investments purchased mainly for the purpose of saving on income taxes. They owned movie tax shelters, Multiple-Unit Residential Buildings (MURBs), flow-through shares, and other investments that had no market value. They had fallen into the trap of buying investments for tax shelter purposes, without concern for whether or not those investments were sound in and of themselves. They were much worse off than if they had simply put their money in the bank and paid their taxes when they were due.

Later, I became a licensed trustee in bankruptcy. In this role, I saw what happens when people spend more than they earn, or become mired in debt by speculating in risky ventures, or try to get ahead financially without a sensible plan.

In the next phase in my career, I worked as a financial advisor in two different major securities firms. It wasn't long before I began to see how the biases that exist in the industry can work against a poorly informed investor. Most of the training I was given was in marketing and selling, not in investing and financial planning. The only requirement to get into the business was to pass the courses to obtain a licence to sell mutual funds. I did this and soon after also completed the certified financial planner (CFP) degree. Through this training, I gained a better perspective on the industry and what it takes for people to attain financial security. Later, after obtaining a securities licence, I gained experience and an even better understanding of markets and financial planning.

The biggest increase in my knowledge came when I completed the certified investment management analyst (CIMA) program. This program, sponsored by the Wharton School of Business, helped me gain a better grasp of how to monitor, measure, and control investment risk. In 2004, in order to understand hedge funds better, I completed the certified hedge fund specialists course (CHSF).

The personal element should not be discounted. Not only have I listened to many, many people in the course of my work, coming to understand their problems and the cause of their problems, but I also have made many of the mistakes I describe in the book.

QUESTIONS FOR YOUR FINANCIAL ADVISOR

Throughout this book, I will be giving you advice on dealing with financial advisors, but for now here are some introductory remarks about them.

I believe that there are two basic types of financial advisors. There are those I call *old school advisors*, who have the objective of beating the market through superior knowledge and active trading. And there are those I call *new school advisors*, whose main objective is to earn the return their clients need to earn, while managing and controlling risk.

In this book, I frequently suggest that you should ask your financial advisor about such things as the level of risk you are taking, the range of returns you should expect, and how large a loss you should expect in a bad year. In all likelihood, only the new school advisors, ones who have taken advanced courses such as those offered in the CFA, CIM, or CIMA programs, or those who have access to optimization software, will be able to answer these questions.

I believe that the most important thing an advisor can do is to monitor and minimize risk. Nothing is as important as protecting capital. There are some very wise and experienced advisors who manage risk by using their common sense, market knowledge, and years of experience. These advisors may not be able to answer questions about risk, standard deviation, correlation ratios, and Sharpe Ratios, but they do consistently minimize risk by using their common sense and good experience. Other advisors, possibly those newer to the profession and thus with less actual trading experience, are more likely to use analytical tools and optimization programs to minimize risk.

My advice to you is to ask about the level of risk in your portfolio and satisfy yourself, one way or another, that your advisor understands your tolerance for risk and is managing risk, either by analytical software programs or by old-fashioned common sense.

WHAT THIS BOOK DOES

The format of this book is very simple. Each part covers a basic aspect of financial planning in a straightforward, common sense manner. Within each part, short sections—called tips—concentrate on a single principle of saving and investing. At the end of each tip is a bottom-line summary of the point and concise advice on what you can do right now. Throughout the book you will find practical advice on working with your financial advisor.

The book does not dispense get-rich-quick advice. Rather, it helps you determine your financial goals, particularly with regard to retirement, maps out a sensible approach for achieving those goals, and warns you of the pitfalls to avoid.

My hope is that the time you spend reading this book will prove to be a wise investment in your financial security and personal well-being.

Part 1

Taking Responsibility
for Your Financial Success

"The investor's chief problem—and even his worst enemy—
is likely to be himself."

Benjamin Graham,
Wall Street legend and proponent of value investing

Tip 1

Recognize the Real Obstacles to Your Financial Security

You will never be financially secure until you understand that the real problems holding you back are probably your own attitudes and misconceptions.

The obstacles that keep us from enjoying financial security are usually not low salaries, too much income tax, stock market crashes, or our own less-than-perfect financial advisors. They are more likely to stem from wrong attitudes and wrong thinking. Some of the obstacles may include

- not taking responsibility for our own financial success;
- not making financial security one of our main goals;
- not knowing what rate of return is needed to achieve our goals;
- not having a financial plan that shows what we must do to achieve our goals;
- getting all our financial advice from salespeople;
- thinking that finances are too complicated to understand;
- not having, and sticking to, an investment strategy; or
- focusing on investment products rather than on the investment process.

Financial security comes to those who want it more than the pleasure they may receive from spur-of-the moment, feel-good purchases. It comes to those who can visualize its benefits and are willing to spend and live within the level of their current income. It comes to those who spend less than they earn and save the difference. Financial security rarely comes to those who try to become wealthy through speculation. You don't have to be lucky or brilliant or earn a high income to become financially secure. You just need to save regularly and avoid the most common investment mistakes.

Financial security and financial independence are not the same thing. Financial security is being on the path that will lead to financial independence. Financial security is a state of mind that gives you a confidence that pays psychological as well as financial dividends. You can have financial security by avoiding simple mistakes and committing to saving 10% of what you earn. Financial independence is having enough income from your pension or your capital to pay your living expenses with no more need to work for a living. Obviously, the more income necessary to support your lifestyle, the more capital you will need and the longer it will take to reach financial independence.

You will achieve financial independence when you take responsibility for your finances and manage your money wisely. If you stick to a sensible plan, financial independence in your old age is virtually certain. To make it happen, however, you must take charge. If you are not on the road to this independence and you are close to retirement, then more drastic measures will be needed. The specific steps required will become clear when you prepare a comprehensive financial plan.

BOTTOM LINE: You can overcome financial difficulties and accumulate enough capital to retire in comfort. The key is to have specific goals and a keen desire to achieve them. When you have goals and they are sufficiently important that you put money aside to achieve them, then the magic of compounding interest will do the rest.

WHAT YOU CAN DO NOW: Start taking control of your own financial security by getting a financial plan that shows what you need to do to become financially independent. When you have a financial plan, you must also want the goals badly enough to continue following the plan. You have to know your goals, take charge, and take action.

Take Responsibility for Your Own Investment Success

You will reach financial independence only if you realize that you are in control and that financial security depends on your commitment to the process.

When it comes to personal finances, we frequently act as if things are beyond our control. In cases where we do not save enough put aside to build financial independence, we may blame our employer for a low salary, the government for taking too much in tax, or the economy for high inflation and interest rates. We may consider it unfair that rent and daycare are so expensive, making it impossible for us to pay for all our day-to-day expenses, let alone have money left over to save.

Similarly, when we experience bad investing results, we blame the markets, the economy, management fees, or income tax. We fault our financial advisor for not picking stocks that always increase in value. We blame our accountant for not helping us avoid more income tax, and our financial planner not giving us a financial plan that keeps us on track.

The point is, however, that we should expect these problems. All of them can be overcome or avoided, however, when we take responsibility for our financial security.

Albert Ellis, the renowned psychotherapist, has said, "Your financial health is a function of the attitudes you have learned and taught yourself about money over the years." We have created our financial situation and we have the power to change it. Just as improving our health requires personal commitment, improving our finances requires that we make financial security one of our priorities.

You must first take responsibility for setting your financial goals. You, or you and your spouse, should sit down and decide what you really want out of life. You almost certainly will not be able to get everything you want. But you are likely to get more of what you want if you agree on what you are aiming for and are willing to work toward it.

If you don't have the knowledge to do this yourself, work with a financial planner to create a financial plan that shows what you must do to achieve your most important goals. When you know the amount you must save, you can adjust your spending to reach that target. Then you can budget for the things you want most: a nice home, education for your children, early retirement, or the ability to help others by leaving a valuable estate.

If you already have a financial advisor, you should still go through this goal-setting exercise with him or her. It is amazing how few advisors actually know their clients' financial history or goals. This is where you can start to work more effectively with your advisor.

Take the time to choose your priorities before spending on things of lesser importance. To get the things that are really important to you, you may have to make some difficult choices. These choices might mean moving to a smaller home, getting by with one car, reducing vacation costs, cutting up your credit cards, buying nothing until you have the cash available, or avoiding expensive restaurants. If you say, "But this is impossible—I don't want to give up any of these things," then your only alternative is to stay in debt, work until you die, and never experience the freedom of money in the bank and the feeling of financial security.

You can't have it both ways. It is impossible to spend more than you earn and still create financial security. Delaying decisions too long will mean even tougher choices in the future. After you have committed yourself to a regular savings program, the next step is to monitor results and ask questions when your investments are not performing as expected. Obtain a basic understanding of how the stock market works. Finish reading this book to get a better grasp of how you can avoid the mistakes that most investors make.

Almost anyone, regardless of investment expertise, present income, and financial circumstances, can become financially secure by following the simple steps listed below. You don't need to be an expert on financial matters to gain financial security. What's needed is the recognition that you are the master of your own destiny.

Do not assume that hiring an advisor frees you from making decisions, setting goals, and monitoring the results. Be involved in the process. Your input is essential. Just as you cannot turn all responsibility for your health and fitness over to a personal fitness trainer, so you cannot turn all of your financial decisions over to your financial advisor. A fitness trainer can show you the exercise, but you still have to do it. It's the same with your finances. Unless your pension plan is generous enough to provide for all your needs and wants in retirement, you will need to save regularly, have a plan that shows the required rate of return, and follow the plan. You must ask questions, make decisions, and monitor the results.

At a minimum, you must

- itemize your major financial goals.
- prioritize your major financial goals.
- get a financial plan that shows how much you need to save to achieve your goals.
- ask your financial advisor for something called an investment policy statement (IPS). An IPS is an agreement between you and your advisor that explains how things are expected to work. (See Tip 9 on pages 21–26 for an in-depth description of this agreement.)
- stick to a simple but sensible investment strategy.
- commit to saving each month the amount your plan calls for.
- spend the time necessary to monitor your investment portfolio.

If the recommendation to live within your present income seems like tough medicine, consider the benefits. Once you turn things around and have a positive cash flow, you can enjoy more material things and spend more on other pursuits than you would be able to if you were to stay in debt.

BOTTOM LINE: Take charge. Don't think of yourself as a victim of circumstances. A change in behaviour will bring a change in results. The process is easier than you think and will bring more pleasure than you can now imagine.

WHAT YOU CAN DO NOW: Finish reading this book to get a basic understanding of what you have to do to achieve financial security.

Tip 3

Don't Think a Higher Income in the Future Will Make Up for a Late Start

If you think that eventually you will make up for a late start by saving more when your income is higher, you are fooling yourself. It will not be any easier to save in the future when you have a higher income. You can save only when you spend less than you earn. In the absence of a commitment to save, a higher income may only mean higher spending.

Many examples show us that the surest way to become financially independent is to start saving at an early age. Ten years of compound interest is a surer route to riches than a plan to invest later in investments that will produce an exceptionally high rate of return.

Typically, the young say that they don't earn enough to start saving. They think that the amount they save is not enough to invest. Thus, many young people tend to forget about accumulating any savings.

Compare the progress of someone who starts to save at 20 with that of someone who starts at 35. After the late starter begins to save, he or she will have to save about four times as much each year to arrive at the same total as the early saver.

Most young people will tell you how difficult it is to save because it costs so much to maintain their lifestyle. Those just beginning family life with children find it especially difficult. Yet it isn't all about the scarcity of money. Many young couples live at a standard just above the limit of what they can afford.

Consider the couple who make a combined income of $80,000 and spend about $81,000 during the year. Chances are that if their combined income were to rise to $100,000, they would spend $102,000, or if it were to go up to $120,000, their spending would increase to $125,000. As soon as this couple's income goes up, their standard of living goes up. They move to a nicer apartment, buy a better car, and take more expensive vacations.

Saving is something this couple plan to do in the future, when their income is higher. They are forgetting one important fact: The key to higher savings is not a higher income; it is the decision to spend less than you earn. Savings can be generated only when there is a commitment to save. Individuals who truly feel the need to save can do so even with very low incomes. Saving is easy if you make the commitment to live within your means.

Young people who do save will find that they have much more to spend in future years, for two reasons: (1) they will not have to spend a large portion of their income on interest on debt, and (2) the interest earned on their savings will be available to spend.

It is possible for almost everyone to live happily on much less. This should be especially encouraging to those who think they just can't save because they need all of their income to live on. Sometimes people have to lose a job or take a lower-paying job before they really learn this lesson.

I once took a 50% cut in my income after leaving a secure position as a manager with a major accounting firm to take up a new position as a commission salesperson. While at the accounting firm, I would never have believed it possible for my wife and I to cut back so drastically. But we did, and we now look back on those belt-tightening years as some of the most enjoyable years of our marriage.

Many excellent books point the way to a lifestyle of good saving habits. By reading just a few of them, you should have as much fun saving money and watching your capital grow as you now are spending money.

To inspire you on the way to savings, here are three good sources: *The Richest Man in Babylon* by George S. Clason, *Your Money or Your Life* by Joe Dominguez and Vicki Robin, and *The Automatic Investor* by David Bach, a state-of-the-art savings guide.

BOTTOM LINE: Many people think that a higher income will make it easier to save more in the future. However, they will find that there will never be surplus money because expenses, if unchecked, will always grow faster than income.

WHAT YOU CAN DO NOW: Decide what changes you have to make to your lifestyle so that you can save 10% of what you earn.

Tip 4

Know Your Target Rate of Return

If you do not know the rate of return that you should be aiming for, you may be taking either too much risk or too little.

To become financially secure, you need to be clear about your goals. When your goals are clear, the financial-planning process will show the rate of return you need to earn on your investments in order to meet your objectives. This rate of return becomes the target against which to measure success or failure.

If you don't have any goals, it doesn't matter what you do with your finances. However, most people do have some idea of what they want. To have meaning, goals must be clear, quantified, and tied to a specific time period. For example, if the plan is based on retirement goals, the first step is to set the retirement date and the amount of money you expect to spend in your retirement years.

Assume, for example, that you want to retire in 20 years. At that time, you want to spend $40,000 per year in today's dollars. Assume that you have $100,000 saved today and you are saving $1,000 per month. Assume also that in retirement you will earn $1,000 per month in pension income. Given reasonable assumptions for inflation, life expectancy, and income tax, you will need a rate of return of about 8% to achieve these goals.

On the other hand, if you are 65, already retired, with $15,000 a year in pension income and $600,000 in RRSPs, and you expect to spend $35,000 per year, with your primary objective being not to run out of money before age 90, then you need to earn only about 5%.

In a well-planned investment portfolio, higher returns require higher risk. More risk is required to earn a return of 8% than a return of 5%. In the above example, since the retired person needs only a 5% rate of return to achieve his objective, it makes no sense to have a higher-risk portfolio designed to make 8% or 10%.

Most investors aim for a higher rate of return than is reasonable to expect for a given level of risk. Most investment advisors are programmed to shoot for the highest return possible while staying within the level of risk that their clients can tolerate. It is not uncommon, therefore, for investors to be in an investment portfolio that has higher risk than necessary. In order to avoid this situation, you should ask about potential risks even before you begin talking about expected returns.

Taking more risk than necessary increases the probability that an unexpected market drop will cause you to lose so much capital that your standard of living will be affected. On the other hand, if you don't take enough risk, your earnings will be too low and you may run out of money in your old age.

The proper steps to establish the rate of return you need to achieve your goals are as follows:

- Clarify your financial goals.
- Get a financial plan that shows what rate of return you need to reach these goals.
- Have your investment portfolio designed to achieve the required rate of return with the least amount of risk possible.
- Monitor your portfolio on a quarterly basis.

BOTTOM LINE: Make sure you have a properly prepared financial plan that shows your target rate of return. If you don't have a target rate of return, you are, in effect, saying to your financial advisor, "Here's my money, do your best, and whatever you do will be okay with me." You wouldn't drive without a speedometer, and you shouldn't invest without establishing a meaningful target rate of return. To achieve financial goals, a wise investor takes as much risk as necessary but no more.

WHAT YOU CAN DO NOW: Get a financial plan that clarifies your goals and shows the rate of return your portfolio needs to earn to achieve those goals. If your financial plan shows you have to earn an average return of over 10% per annum, then you have to go back to the drawing board. In the present economic environment, it is simply not realistic to expect consistent double-digit returns over a long period of time.

Part 2

Choosing and Working with a Financial Advisor

"There was a time when clients trusted professionals automatically . . . Sound character and reputation were assumed, and business was conducted with confidence . . . Although that world may be gone, the need for trust has not disappeared."

David H. Maister, Charles H. Green, Robert M. Galford,
in *The Trusted Advisor*

Tip 5

Use the Right Strategy to Select a Financial Advisor

You are unlikely to achieve financial peace of mind if your financial advisor does not understand or agree with your goals and is unwilling to consider or discuss your investment concerns.

Investors looking to choose or change a financial advisor usually decide to go with the first prospective advisor they interview. After the first meeting, they are sold on the financial advisor's abilities, personality, and knowledge. There should be no surprise here; financial advisors have to be effective salespeople or they would soon go out of business. Naturally, they are going to be skillful in addressing your concerns and making you feel comfortable about opening an investment account with them.

To give yourself a fighting chance of finding a financial advisor who will match your needs, you should interview at least three candidates. Look at each advisor's educational background. Is the prospective advisor qualified at only the minimum level, entitling her to sell only mutual funds? Does she have a financial-planning designation, or a more advanced financial certification such as certified financial planner (CFP), Canadian investment manager (CIM), chartered financial analyst (CFA), chartered life underwriter (CLU), or certified investment management analyst (CIMA)? All things being equal, the more degrees and educational certificates, the better.

Examine the advisor's level of experience. Ideally, you want an advisor with at least 10 years of experience. It takes about that much time for advisors to learn from the mistakes they will make early in their careers. Only experience can train an advisor to keep a cool head in the midst of market turmoil, to resist the sales pressure during the weekly visits from mutual fund and hedge fund wholesalers, and to understand how highly touted packaged deals can backfire. Don't choose an advisor who's going to learn the ropes with your money. (I can say for certain that the advice I give my clients today is better than the advice I was able to give when I was new to the industry.)

Avoid choosing a financial advisor who is too successful to find time for you. This might mean a person who only handles accounts much larger than yours or one who already has over 500 clients.

Find out what size of accounts the advisor specializes in and how many clients he has. Keep away from someone who is so new he is desperate to start generating enough income to keep his job. Financial advisors sometimes are exposed to temptations to earn commissions in ways that may not be in the client's best interest. The desire to earn commissions may result in recommendations that benefit the advisor more than the client.

Education and experience are more important than the advisor's personality. You are not selecting an advisor to find a new friend. Rather, you want one who will manage your funds to earn the rate of return you need while taking no more risk than necessary.

Here are some key questions to ask your prospective advisor:

- What is your educational background? What relevant professional degrees do you have?
- How many years have you been in the industry, in what positions, and with what firms? (Ask to see a résumé.)
- What is your investment philosophy and how do you put investment portfolios together?
- Do you prepare a financial plan to determine the rate of return needed in order to achieve your client's goals, or do you always go for the highest return possible?
- How do you manage and control risk?
- Do you use investment policy statements and, if so, may I see one?
- How many clients do you have?
- What is the size of your average client's portfolio?
- What fees do you charge?

BOTTOM LINE: Choosing an advisor is an important decision. Spend enough time on the selection process to be confident that you have the right match.

WHAT YOU CAN DO NOW: Arm yourself with the questions listed above and begin the interviewing process. With these questions answered, you are going to have the knowledge necessary to find the right advisor.

Tip 6

Don't Ignore the Signs that You Should Change Advisors

Not every financial advisor is as experienced, honest, and competent as you might wish. If you have the wrong advisor, you may have to work a lot longer before you can retire—or you will have much less to spend in your retirement.

It is never wise to rush to change financial advisors. When you think a change is needed, the first step should be to explain your concerns to your current advisor. The source of conflict could be a misunderstanding. Making a fresh start with a new financial plan and a new investment policy statement (see pages 21–26) could get you back on track with less cost and pain than switching advisors.

On the other hand, incompetent advisors count on your wanting to avoid the pain, aggravation, and expense of changing advisors. If changing were easy, they might lose many clients. Nevertheless, sometimes the match is just not right. In such a case, the prudent thing to do is to make the change. Here are examples of situations that should prompt you to change advisors:

- There is evidence of dishonesty.
- There is evidence that recommendations are not in your best interests (an example might be frequent trading recommendations).
- The advisor keeps on recommending individual stocks even though her recommendations have underperformed the benchmark index for the past three years. (In this case you would be better off using something called an exchange-traded fund [ETF]; see Part 9.)
- The financial advisor does not agree to some form of an investment policy statement providing a clear benchmark against which his performance can be measured.
- Actual performance is outside the range of expected results, and the advisor does not have a satisfactory explanation of what went wrong.
- There is evidence that the advisor is learning the ropes by handling your account.

Changing advisors is a serious decision, but not changing advisors could mean working for a few years longer than you planned. The wrong strategy could wipe out—in a single year—20% or more of the value of your portfolio. Depending on your age, it may be difficult to recover from a loss of this magnitude. In making a decision to stay with a financial advisor, you must be mindful of the possible negative consequences. After one loss, you could lose even more if things continue to go wrong. In a bad portfolio and in a bear market, the losses can continue year after year. The financial advisor may lose a client, but you may lose your financial security.

BOTTOM LINE: Some client–advisor relationships are intolerable. If you find yourself in such a situation, you should make a change. If you don't, you may have to work longer before you can retire.

WHAT YOU CAN DO NOW: Read the relevant parts in this book, talk to your financial advisor, and make an informed decision about whether or not a change is required.

Tip 7

Understand Your Advisor's Investment Strategy

Most investors do not have a strategy that they follow consistently in both up markets and down markets. Yet the most important element in ensuring investing success is having the discipline to stick with the chosen investment strategy.

Does your financial advisor have a well-reasoned investment philosophy that is suited to your needs? You should not assume that every financial advisor follows an investment strategy that makes sense for your portfolio.

Every advisor has an investment strategy of some kind. In the worst case, it might involve "churning" the client's account to make the highest possible fees. Other bad strategies include switching investments to what is hot at the moment; buying based on recommendations made on TV stock market shows; buying all of the brokerage firm's current choices, or all the new issues; or buying on hunches and the belief that the advisor can beat the market.

The point is to understand the strategy and stick with it through different market and economic cycles. Many strategies will work well. The key to success in almost every case is to stay with the strategy through the bad times as well as the good.

Alarms should go off in your head if your financial advisor is unable to explain his investment strategy in terms that you can understand. The bells are telling you that it may be time to switch to a new advisor.

An advisor who has a strategy has thought things through and knows why certain investments are purchased at certain times. She has a plan that looks forward and anticipates changes. Beware of the advisor who is prone to go with her emotions. Buying and selling securities based on emotion is a sure way to lose capital.

BOTTOM LINE: Your financial advisor should have a well-thought-out investment strategy that can be explained in terms a layperson can understand.

WHAT YOU CAN DO NOW: Get an explanation of your financial advisor's investment strategy and an opinion on why it is the best strategy for you. Make sure you find out how the proposed plan will be useful in minimizing risk for the expected return. Make sure you understand how the strategy is expected to work in good markets and bad.

Identify Your Advisor's Area of Expertise

You and your financial advisor must be on the same page in terms of strategy and investment philosophy.

Different financial advisors will recommend very different approaches, reflecting different outlooks on the markets and different levels of experience and expertise.

For instance, advisors who are bond specialists will tend to believe that a diversified portfolio of bonds is the best investment. Advisors who have had success in picking mid-sized Canadian resource companies will tend to suggest investing in such companies. Other advisors may believe they can do better for you than the market average by investing in a few large-capitalization growth companies. Still others develop an expertise in selecting mutual funds, hedge funds, income trusts, and structured investment products.

If your financial advisor is one of these specialists but you believe the best approach is to own a widely diversified portfolio consisting of stocks, exchange-traded funds, bonds, hedge funds, and income trusts, the two of you are likely to be in constant conflict.

An advisor's recommendations will tend to reflect his or her level of professional education and experience. A highly trained advisor with experience of both bull and bear markets is more likely to offer you well-informed advice, which is especially valuable in hard times. Some financial advisors are generalists and see the big picture but choose to leave the details to associates. Others know the details and history of different stocks but offer no assessment of the overall stock market and economy. Many experienced advisors accept only clients who agree with their recommended strategies.

Advisors starting out in the business need clients and will tend to take on every new prospect. In effect, they are trying to be all things to all people. I made this mistake in my early years. On occasion, I accepted clients who wanted a service that I wasn't comfortable providing. They thought that my role was to beat the market by actively trading Canadian stocks. I saw this as an impractical objective. I believed that the advisor's role was to help achieve the client's objectives by designing a portfolio that could be expected to earn the necessary return with the least possible amount of risk. If these clients had asked more questions at the outset, and if I had followed my instincts, many misunderstandings could have been avoided.

Before making a decision to select an advisor, you should know his or her strengths, weaknesses, expertise, and beliefs about investing. You should ask the basic questions regarding

- areas of expertise;
- relevant investment experience;
- investment philosophy and strategy;
- the method used to determine the asset mix and strategy that is right for each client;
- how often the advisor recommends changes in the account; and
- what makes the financial advisor believe she is better than the average advisor.

BOTTOM LINE: You can avoid problems by staying away from advisors who, because of their limited investment experience, want to slot you into an investment portfolio that does not fit your style of investing. The value of a client-centred investment policy statement (IPS), as described in Tip 9, which follows, is that the strategy is in writing and both parties can easily refer to it.

WHAT YOU CAN DO NOW: Ask your financial advisor to (1) explain the investment strategy that he recommends; (2) review the main risks involved with the strategy; and (3) explain why he thinks this is the best strategy for you.

Get an Investment Policy Statement

A client-centred investment policy statement (IPS) is one of the best ways to establish guidelines for your portfolio's performance.

One way to increase the chances of a profitable and harmonious relationship with your financial advisor is to develop an agreed-upon investment policy statement (IPS).

With an IPS both you and your advisor are clear on your goals, the strategy to achieve them, and the yardstick for measuring success. With this tool you can discuss the performance of your investment portfolio calmly and rationally. There will be no need to argue when it comes time to evaluate performance. The IPS helps measure whether or not your portfolio has performed within the expected range of returns.

A custom-prepared, client-centred IPS is quite different from a "boilerplate" IPS designed to protect the investment firm and to satisfy the industry's injunction to advisors to know their clients. The boilerplate IPS is often written in language that makes it difficult for the client to measure performance.

The following is an example of what should be covered in a client-centred IPS.

INVESTMENT POLICY STATEMENT

The purpose of this investment policy statement is to set out in clear terms

1. the target average rate of return for this investment portfolio over different time periods; e.g., the target return over any one-year period, any three-year period, or any ten-year period;
2. the expected range of returns for the portfolio as a whole over different time periods; e.g., for any one-year period, the range between the best likely result and the worst likely result;
3. the starting percentages in each asset class in the recommended portfolio and the permissible ranges for each asset class;

4. the benchmark that will be used to evaluate actual performance;
5. investment constraints, if any;
6. the rebalancing strategy;
7. all fees that will be charged;
8. frequency of contact;
9. topics to be covered in the quarterly review meeting; and
10. assumptions being made about performance of investments.

Now let's look at each one of these 10 points in detail, choosing a particular strategy for the sake of discussion.

1. The target rate of return

Let's say the target rate of return is 8% per annum. It is understood that in some years the portfolio will give a higher return than 8% and in some years it will give a lower return than 8%. It is expected, however, that if the portfolio consistently performs within the expected range of returns as shown below, the actual return, over time, will be close to the target rate of return.

2. The expected range of returns may be similar to what is shown below

	1 yr	3 yrs	5 yrs	10 yrs
Highest expected return	24	18	14	12
Average expected return	8	8	8	8
Lowest expected return	−6	−2	3	4

The portfolio is constructed so that 95 times out of 100, the actual return is expected to fall within the above ranges. This means that 2.5 times out of 100, the actual portfolio performance is expected to be worse than the lowest expected return, and 2.5 times out of 100, the actual portfolio performance is expected to be better than the highest expected return.

3. The initial allocation

The initial allocation to different asset classes included in this portfolio, and the permissible ranges, are as follows:

Asset Class	Initial Allocation	Permissible Range
Cash	5%	0–10%
Government bonds	25%	15–35%
Other fixed income	15%	5–30%
Canadian equities	15%	5–30%
Foreign equities	15%	5–30%
Income trusts	10%	5–15%
Multi-strategy hedge funds	15%	10–25%

It is assumed that the asset allocation will be designed to be efficient from both an income tax and a risk-minimization point of view. Optimization will be used in order to develop an overall mix that is near or on what's called the *efficient frontier*. (Optimization is the process whereby asset classes are selected to minimize risk for any given level of return.)

4. The benchmark

For the above asset mix, the portfolio benchmark might be a portfolio made up of indexes in the following percentages:

Government of Canada T-bills	5%
Scotia McLeod Short-Term Bond Index	40%
S&P/TSX Composite Index	25%
S&P 500 Index	15%
Hennessee Hedge Fund Index	15%

(If the hypothetical portfolio made up of these indexes produced a return of 7%, you would want to do at least as well, after fees.)

5. Investment constraints

Some portfolios may be constructed with investment constraints: for example, all bonds must be government bonds, or 50% of the portfolio must be invested in Canada, or all investments in emerging markets are to be avoided.

6. The rebalancing strategy

Over time, some asset classes will rise in value while others decline. Rebalancing will be required to bring the portfolio back to the desired asset allocation. Rebalancing involves selling some assets that have risen in value and buying more assets that have fallen in value. The portfolio will normally be rebalanced annually. However, if the percentage in any asset class or the cumulative change from all asset classes changes by more than 10% of the value of the portfolio as a whole, the advisor will discuss the possibility of rebalancing more frequently to take advantage of the opportunity to sell high and buy low.

7. Fees and advisor compensation

Fees include any commissions, wrap account fees, service fees, management expense ratios (MERs), administration fees, front-end fees, deferred sales charges. (A wrap account is a fee-based account in which a number of services are all "wrapped" or "bundled" into a single fee.)

Advisor compensation may include trading commissions, trailer fees, program management fees, fees from deferred sales charges, and new issue commissions.

The IPS should show the total of all fees (in dollars or as a percentage of assets) that the client will pay, as well as the total compensation earned by the financial advisor. It is important for the client to be aware of both the amount he or she pays and the amount the advisor receives from other sources.

8. Frequency of contact

The IPS might indicate, for example, that on a quarterly basis the financial advisor will make a telephone contact to review performance and any issues that have come up; that on an annual basis there will be a face-to-face meeting to discuss the issues set out in the formal meeting agenda; and that on an as-needed basis the client will call in regarding administrative issues and speak to an assistant and the assistant will discuss the issues with the advisor as appropriate.

9. Topics to be covered in formal review meetings

On a quarterly basis, the client will receive a report that highlights actual performance compared against the target range of returns and the benchmark return.

The first purpose of the quarterly review is to determine whether the actual return fell within the expected range of returns. If it did not, your advisor should be able to tell you which of the following reasons explain the deviation:

- There was a once-in-a-lifetime event that caused markets to move outside the range of returns expected to occur 95% of the time.
- The selected investments did not perform like their representative class.
- The original range for the portfolio as a whole was calculated incorrectly. Any or all of the following may have been miscalculated: the historical rate of return, the standard deviation of the asset classes, or the correlation between asset classes.
- Other factors (which your advisor should specifically identify). The second purpose of the quarterly review is to determine how the portfolio performed as compared with the benchmark portfolio. Even if the performance of the portfolio was within the expected range, that does not necessarily mean that performance could not be improved. If the actual performance of the individual asset classes and the performance as a whole are significantly different from the benchmark, this may mean that individual asset classes or mutual funds should be changed.

Topics that should be covered at the annual meeting include

- fees charged during the period;
- provision of an annual capital gains and losses report for income tax purposes; and
- a review to determine whether the level of volatility is acceptable—is the client sleeping well at night?

10. Assumptions

Your advisor is operating under certain assumptions about the perform-ance of investments, including the rate of inflation, marginal tax rates, and the schedule for withdrawals. These assumptions should be listed and explained.

BOTTOM LINE: When large financial institutions, such as pension plans, foun-dations, or university endowment funds, hire investment managers, they always have an IPS in place. This ensures a good and effective relationship. Individuals should also have an IPS to make sure that expectations are reasonable and performance is evaluated objectively.

WHAT YOU CAN DO NOW: Ask your financial advisor for a client-centred investment policy statement.

Tip 10
Use the Right Benchmark to Measure Performance

If you don't have the proper tool to measure performance, a performance problem may persist. Your benchmark is the level of performance that you and your advisor agree is necessary and achievable. This is your tool for measuring and monitoring investment performance.

Recognizing a problem with your investment account is the first step toward correcting the situation. The problem can't be fixed until it is identified. You also need a standard by which to measure the dimensions of the problem. This standard is the benchmark: the performance level that you and your advisor agree should be expected from your investment portfolio. The benchmark describes the expected average return and also the expected range of returns for the portfolio. For example, the return benchmark might be an average of 8% over five years, and the range-of-return benchmark might be between –5% and +15%. Comparing your performance against the wrong benchmark may lead you to think you are doing well when, in fact, you are doing poorly.

From a financial advisor's point of view, the oldest trick in the book is to make a client feel good by comparing performance with the wrong benchmark. To avoid this problem, you and your advisor should agree in advance on how performance will be measured and what reference points will be used in making comparisons. When the advisor agrees to use a specific benchmark, several good outcomes will follow:

- The advisor will be accountable for results.
- There will be no way to conceal underperformance of the portfolio.
- Whether or not the portfolio has underperformed can be determined without an emotional confrontation.
- The advisor will have an incentive to keep fees low because performance numbers will be reduced by the amount of fees charged.
- The asset mix will be reassessed regularly for its efficiency.
- The financial advisor will be on notice that fudging of results is not an option.

Not having an agreed-upon benchmark creates several problems. For example, assume you have an investment portfolio made up of 50% Canadian common stocks and 50% government bonds. Your account statements show that over the past three years, your return averaged 3% per annum. You tell your financial advisor that you think that with this asset mix you should be doing much better. Your financial advisor is shocked and explains that you have in fact done very well. As evidence, she points out that over the past five years the S&P/TSX Composite Index has been down by 10%, the NASDAQ by 30%, and the MSCI Emerging Markets Index by 20%. She explains that, since these three markets are down by an average of 20%, her efforts have resulted in your earning at least a 23% improvement over the average return in the equity markets. If you accept this line of reasoning, you are being seriously misled:

- You are not 100% invested in the equity markets, so the comparison is misleading. Let's say your portfolio is a blend of 50% Canadian stocks and 50% Canadian government bonds. The performance benchmark, therefore, should be based on the average of these two specific indexes, and not on unrelated indexes.
- You are not invested in the NASDAQ or in emerging markets so the performance of these markets is irrelevant.
- The advisor has compared your three-year return with the five-year return on the various indexes. Not only should she use the proper index but she also should use identical time periods. Comparisons are always misleading when they are not for precisely the same period.

The foregoing is an example of a "relative return" benchmark for judging the performance of a financial advisor or investment manager. Here, you are comparing your return against the external benchmark that you and your advisor have agreed is the proper one. (The benchmark should be agreed upon in advance, not after the fact.) However, another yardstick, the *absolute return*, is even more important. This yardstick is the rate of return you need to earn to reach your financial goals. You should be aware of how actual performance compares against both benchmarks.

On a relative return basis, if you lose 12% but the benchmark lost 20%, you might (in theory) feel satisfied because you "beat the benchmark." The reality, however, is that investors don't like to lose money—even if they have lost less than the benchmark index. With an absolute return benchmark, if you need to earn 10% to achieve your goals, you want a portfolio designed to earn 10% on average. You don't care what happens in the stock market, you care only that you are earning, on average, the rate of return you need.

You should understand, however, that even with an absolute return benchmark of, say, 8%, you are not going to earn 8% every year without fail. If your plan calls for an average return of 8%, your actual return in any given year will almost always be either higher or lower than the long-term average. You should know the expected range of returns for your portfolio and you should always be within the expected range of returns regardless of what happens to the market in a particular year.

BOTTOM LINE: Don't let your financial advisor make bad or mediocre performance look good by comparing your performance results against the wrong benchmark. Agreeing in advance to the use of the proper benchmarks will help prevent arguments about performance levels.

A relative return benchmark is used to judge your financial advisor's performance while an absolute return benchmark tells you if you are on track to achieve your financial goals.

WHAT YOU CAN DO NOW: Talk to your financial advisor and get his agreement on the benchmark that will be used to judge performance. Check out the website *www.showmethebenchmark.ca*.

Don't Expect Your Financial Advisor to Beat the Market

When you try to beat the market, you increase your trading costs, take more risk, and make yourself vulnerable when – not if – he next major market correction occurs.

The old school image of the financial advisor is of someone who understands the market and employs experience, insights, intelligence, and research to choose stocks that rise in value by more than the market as a whole. Logic, common sense, and the Internet will tell you that this image no longer fits today's financial advisors, if it ever did. If an advisor were able to purchase stocks that consistently yield a higher return than the market's average (without higher than average market risk), he would use that skill to become one of the world's richest investors himself.

It is simply unrealistic for you to expect your financial advisor to consistently beat the market. After all, only a minority of professional portfolio managers achieve results better than the market index, and they have greater resources than most advisors. These managers spend much of their time making investment decisions, while the average financial advisor spends more time being of service to clients, trying to attract new ones, and dealing with administrative issues. It is unrealistic that your advisor will beat the market consistently without taking higher than normal market risk.

The advisor can still provide an important service: helping you determine the rate of return you need and designing a portfolio that brings solid returns with the least possible amount of risk. That said, there are some advisors who do consistently beat the market. By this I mean they earn a higher rate of return than could be earned by simply buying an index mutual fund. There may also be some cases where the advisor not only beats the market, but also does so with lower than normal market risk. In most cases, however, higher than average returns are possible only when higher than average risk is taken.

BOTTOM LINE: Most dissatisfaction between client and advisor arises from unrealistic expectations about what the financial advisor can actually do.

WHAT YOU CAN DO NOW: Talk to your financial advisor so that you are both clear on the benchmark for the account, in terms of the expected average rate of return and level of volatility.

Tip 12

Don't Expect Your Financial Advisor to Get You out of the Market before the Next Crash

Investors who believe their advisor will get them out of the market before a serious crash occurs may allow themselves to be in a riskier portfolio than would otherwise be the case.

It is a huge mistake to think that your advisor is going to be able to protect you from the next market crash (and the question is *when* the next market crash will occur, not whether there will be one). As long as markets continue to move based on the emotions of fear and greed, crashes will occur from time to time.

There are a number of reasons why you should not count on getting a call from your advisor recommending that you sell at the top of the current market cycle:

- It is unlikely that your financial advisor will be able to see a crash coming.
- Even if your advisor wanted to alert her clients, there would not be enough time to call them all.
- Even if your advisor believed that a crash was likely, she would be reluctant to predict the sky is falling: being wrong on this score would seriously reduce her credibility with clients and peers.
- Usually clients don't blame an advisor for a crash when everyone has lost money, but they do blame an advisor if she gets them out of the market too soon and they miss a lot of growth. For this reason, it is safer for the advisor not to try to predict the market.
- If a crash does occur, it will happen when most market participants are experiencing the highest level of optimism. That being the case, even if clients do receive a call, few will accept the advice to get out of the market just at the time when all their neighbours are enthusiastically jumping in.

Here is another reason that you are unlikely to get a call from your advisor suggesting that you bail out. After the first serious downturn, the consensus will be that it is now too late to get out. Everyone will think that the damage has already occurred and the best strategy is to buy more, not to sell when prices are low. Sometimes, after the market falls precipitously, it is a good time to buy. At other times, a sudden drop is just the beginning of a long bear market.

All we know for sure is that markets move in cycles and that it is difficult to predict short-term market movements. The best way to reduce risk is to be diversified across a number of asset classes (i.e., more than just stocks and bonds) that do not all move in the same direction at the same time.

BOTTOM LINE: Do not delude yourself by thinking that your financial advisor is going to call you to let you know before a market crash happens.

WHAT YOU CAN DO NOW: Ask your advisor to estimate how your investment portfolio would be affected if we had another market crash such as occurred in 1929 and 1987.

Tip 13

Avoid Pushing Too Hard and Expecting Unreasonable Results

If you demand a high return, your financial advisor can meet your expectations only by taking higher risks – risks that you may not fully understand.

Investors often have unrealistic expectations of what their investment portfolio should earn and the degree of risk or volatility associated with these earnings. This can cause a problem if investors are forceful in expressing their expectations. To please such a client, an inexperienced advisor will allow himself to be pushed into recommending an asset mix that has the potential for high losses as well as high returns.

Investors rarely recognize that they are in a speculative investment portfolio until the portfolio drops by 20% or 30%. Investors should understand that an investment portfolio that can go up by 20% in one year can, and most likely will, fall by an equal amount in another year.

If you stick with the traditional portfolio made up of stocks and bonds, there are only a few ways that the advisor can reasonably expect to increase the average annual return. One way is by using leverage. Another is by moving to more speculative investments. Yet another is by increasing the concentration in a few securities. In these situations, an investor may earn higher returns in a bull market but the losses may be magnified in a bear market.

Some financial advisors are reluctant to tell you the truth about what you can realistically expect to earn. They are not necessarily dishonest; rather, they fear that, if you knew the truth, you would move your money to another advisor promising a higher return. When you push your advisor and complain about your rate of return, you increase the likelihood that she will recommend higher-risk strategies in an effort to please. As a general rule, you should not expect that your advisor is going to be able to consistently outperform the appropriate benchmark, unless she takes higher risk.

The following chart shows what might be considered a reasonable expectation for the range of returns, based on the last 25 years, for a traditional investment portfolio that is 50% invested in Canadian and US stocks and 50% invested in short- and long-term government bonds.

Range of returns for	any 1-year period	any 3-year period	any 5-year period	any 10-year period	any 20-year period
Best likely	24%	19%	16%	14%	12%
Expected	8%	8%	8%	8%	8%
Worst likely	–5%	–2%	1%	3%	5%

You would expect to hit the high and low ends of this range only once every 20 years. The actual return will be higher than the average return half the time and lower the other half. Yet it is tempting to assume, and many investors do, that annual returns will be above the average more frequently than below it. Statistically, this is unlikely. If you deduct the 2% to 3% that is paid in management fees and commissions, the actual average net return is probably lower than the indicated average expected return.

The chart above shows that the range of expected returns for any one year is quite large, but as you look at longer time periods, the range of expected returns becomes smaller. Quite simply, the range for a 10-year period is lower because, even in the best decade, a few bad years will reduce gains.

The 17-year bull market between 1982 and 1999 had the effect of raising investor expectations. A more realistic view of likely returns for the next 20 years is offered by the investment history of the past 200 years. In that span, seven major bull markets and seven major bear markets occurred. (Bull or bear markets can be measured not only in how the price of shares move up or down but also in how valuations such as the price–earnings ratio move up or down). Using the price–earnings ratio as the measurement, we can see that during the last 200 years, the average bull market lasted about 14 years and the average bear market lasted about 13 years. Given that history, and given that the period from 1982 to 1999 produced unusually high returns, it is unrealistic to expect that a balanced investment portfolio will earn as much during the next 20 years. Over 200 years of history, we see that periods of higher-than-average returns were followed by periods of lower-than-average returns. Experienced investors, like Warren Buffett, are predicting that equity markets will generate returns in the single digits for at least the next decade.

BOTTOM LINE: Don't be greedy. Base your expectations of return on 100 years of history for the investments in your asset class. Don't push your financial advisor to produce a return that is rarely ever attained. Get a financial plan that shows the rate of return you need to earn and aim for that return, not a higher one.

WHAT YOU CAN DO NOW: Ask your financial advisor what rate of return you can reasonably expect from your portfolio. Also ask what the expected range of returns will be. What is the worst likely performance over any one-year period?

Don't Just Delegate Decision-Making; Monitor Results, Too

Delegating without monitoring is, in effect, asking your advisor to be a judge of her own performance. The best way to monitor performance is by using a client-centred investment policy statement.

Investment opportunities are so complicated today that even experienced financial advisors are challenged to keep up to date and to understand the new, complex structured investment products that are available.

It is wise, therefore, to delegate this type of research to your financial advisor. But it is always unwise to delegate without carefully monitoring performance and accepting responsibility for the results. Don't do what most investors do: assume that the control of the portfolio, to all intents and purposes, is out of their hands. You can have the best of both worlds by monitoring your portfolio's performance while benefiting from professional financial advice.

Based on the difference in returns between highly monitored portfolios like those of university endowment funds, and the returns of the average investor, it is reasonable to assume that a properly monitored portfolio will outperform an unwatched portfolio by more than 2% per year. (Note: The assumption that a properly monitored portfolio will outperform a portfolio that is not well managed is based on the historical fact that investment pools such as pension plans, endowment funds, and university trusts typically outperform the relevant benchmarks by about 4% per annum, while the average investor underperforms these benchmarks by about the same amount. I'm being very conservative in stating that a monitored portfolio outperforms an unmanaged portfolio by 2% per annum.)

Monitoring a portfolio simply means

- agreeing with your financial advisor on reasonable goals for volatility and performance;
- comparing actual results with expected results;
- having some understanding of the strategy that is being employed;

- asking for an explanation when results are outside the expected range of results; and
- being aware of the fees that you are paying on your portfolio.

Financial security begins with an understanding that you are responsible for your own financial well-being. Your financial advisor, your insurance agent, and your accountant are all professionals who can help you reach your goals, but you are the one who is ultimately responsible. It is impractical to think that their efforts alone will make you financially secure. And these professionals should not be asked to monitor or judge their own performance.

Monitoring performance mainly means asking questions and expecting reasonable answers. Here are examples of acceptable and unacceptable explanations for underperformance.

Acceptable explanations for portfolio performance outside the range of expected returns:

- The market crashed, dropping in value by more than 25% in the space of one month.
- A terrorist attack caused the stock market to be closed for a week.
- An earthquake caused California to slide into the Pacific Ocean.

Unacceptable explanations for portfolio performance outside the range of expected returns:

- Markets have been down for the year to date.
- Interest rates rose unexpectedly.
- The fund manager was fired for fraud.
- Consumer confidence fell.
- The Canadian dollar rose or fell unexpectedly.

The foregoing unacceptable explanations are normal, expected market events. Your advisor can reduce the risk of these events by diversifying your portfolio.

BOTTOM LINE: You have to monitor performance. This is easy to do when you have an investment policy statement and a clear understanding of the expected range of results (regardless of what happens in the markets). A quick look at your IPS will tell you whether the actual results are outside the expected range of results. If they are, you need an explanation.

WHAT YOU CAN DO NOW: If you do not have a client-centred IPS, call your advisor and ask for one. Then monitor your portfolio to see how it performs compared with the agreed-upon benchmarks for risk and return.

Tip 15

Ask Your Advisor the Tough Questions

Your investment strategy can be compromised if you become so friendly with your financial advisor that you don't feel comfortable asking tough questions.

Financial advisors are fortunate that most investors want to be agreeable. Being friendly and likeable, however, does not always lead to better service. In fact, the most knowledgeable and demanding clients are likely to get the best performance, the lowest fees, and the most phone calls. Of course, there are limits. Good advisors will drop clients who are unreasonable or too demanding. All clients, however, should expect good service, regular contact, and answers to pertinent questions.

Sometimes the client is so easygoing that the financial advisor begins to assume that the client will stay as a client regardless of performance and service. You don't want to be in this situation. There are occasions when a financial advisor needs to call every client to suggest an important change, and you want to be one of the first ones he calls, not one of the last. You want to be a client the advisor wants to impress, not one he takes for granted.

For example, assume that the difference in performance is 1% per annum between the portfolio that the advisor monitors carefully and the one owned by a client that he takes for granted. The latter client is paying a 1% penalty for being so good-natured and undemanding. Being taken for granted, and not receiving information about a better asset mix, could result in your having to work longer before you retire or having to live on a lower income during retirement.

To ensure that you are not taken for granted, you should seek answers to the questions below. (If you have an investment policy statement, most of these questions are already answered.)

- What is the expected return on this portfolio over one, three, five, and ten years?
- What is the worst likely performance over one, three, five, and ten years, based on a 95% confidence level?

- What is the grand total of all the fees I will be paying on this portfolio?
- What investment strategy or rationale is this portfolio based on?
- What is the benchmark against which we will compare performance?
- What is the rebalancing strategy?
- Can we put an investment policy statement in place that will set down in writing the strategies and expectations for this portfolio?

Most of the more experienced and highly qualified financial advisors want their clients to have a comprehensive IPS because this helps investors understand how portfolios can be expected to perform during the bad years. During the occasional bad year, these advisors will receive fewer calls from nervous clients.

BOTTOM LINE: Your financial advisor will treat you with more respect and work more diligently on your account when he knows that you are fair but expect a high standard of performance. When your advisor expects tough but fair questions, he will prepare for meetings and work harder to see that no opportunity is overlooked. You earn this respect when you insist on a written investment policy statement and on getting complete answers to all reasonable questions.

WHAT YOU CAN DO NOW: If you do not already have an investment policy statement, you should call your financial advisor and ask for a meeting to put an IPS in place.

Tip 16
Hold Your Advisor Accountable for Results

The squeaky wheel gets the grease.

There are times when we are almost sure to complain—for instance, if our cars don't work properly after servicing or an appliance goes on the fritz. Yet we rarely hold our financial advisors responsible for a specific level of performance. We assume that the advisor does not control the stock market and therefore cannot control the risk or the return of the investment portfolio.

This is the wrong way to look at the situation. While the advisor does not control the stock market, she can increase or reduce the risk of the portfolio. The advisor can do this by recommending a larger or smaller allocation to the higher-risk part of the investment portfolio. She can also reduce risk by recommending investments that have a low correlation with each other. For instance, she can select investments where the loss on one is normally offset by the gain on another.

You want to take no more risk than the minimum level necessary to achieve the average return that your financial plan shows is necessary to reach your financial goals. A competent financial advisor can put together a portfolio that can be expected to earn your required rate of return, within an agreed-upon, predetermined range of results. The expected range of results—agreed to by advisor and client—will be part of the investment policy statement. A good advisor will also tell you whether or not your "required" rate of return is realistic.

If you decide you want a higher average rate of return, the range of possible returns will also be higher (good years will be better and bad years will be even worse). The range of returns, although higher, is still predictable. There should be very few surprises in a properly designed portfolio. It may perform near the bottom of the range, the middle, or the top, but you can anticipate that 95% of the time the actual results will be within the expected range.

As a client, you are owed a sound explanation for results outside the expected range. The advisor is not liable for any losses, but the explanation should be reasonable. It is not enough just to say that results are poor because the markets were down this year. All advisors know that markets have good years and bad years. A properly designed portfolio will make allowances for this fluctuation. In a bad year, the performance may be near the bottom of the expected range, but the return should not be significantly lower than what was expected in the worst likely year.

The advisor should not be able to escape accountability by providing such a wide estimate of volatility that results are bound to fall within the predicted range. The advisor who says that it is impossible to predict the market, and that your overall portfolio, therefore, might be up or down by 50%, may be trying to avoid being held accountable.

In one way, your relationship with your financial advisor is like your relationship with your spouse. You need good communication. If something is bothering you, the issue should not be allowed to fester; it should be discussed.

BOTTOM LINE: Your financial advisor should be able to design an investment portfolio in which the results fall within a predicted range. Holding your advisor accountable means that you demand a reasonable explanation if results are outside the expected range. A loss outside the expected range should not be explained away simply by saying it was a bad year for the market.

WHAT YOU CAN DO NOW: Ask your financial advisor for an IPS that shows what range of returns your portfolio could be expected to yield over one, three, five, and ten years.

Tip 17

Understand the Biases of the Financial Industry

It is risky to think the industry is on your side, because to some degree investing is like a competition. If you don't know the way the other side plays the game, you are at a serious disadvantage.

Joseph Nocera , writing in *Fortune* magazine, has said that "a broker with a clientele full of contented customers was—and is—a broker who will soon be looking for a new job. Brokers need trades to make money." The banks and brokerage firms that form the backbone of the investment industry need profits to survive. They look on you, the investor, as a potential source of profit. Enlightened self-interest on their part ensures that, for the most part, they will treat you fairly, but a company that doesn't make profits is soon out of business.

One source of profit, of course, is the commissions on transactions generated in your account. In a commission-based account, the brokerage firm and the financial advisor both make more money when the client trades frequently. Obviously, this can create a temptation for your advisor to make more trades than necessary. Excessive trading is called "churning," and fortunately it happens infrequently. Although your advisor may offer a plausible reason for frequent trading (such as recent performance), the real reason is that the purchase of the new position results in additional commissions being earned.

Some investors' accounts are charged a management fee instead of commissions. In these cases, the company earns revenues by managing investment assets. In this type of account, the brokerage firm receives a fee that is usually between 0.5% and 1.5% of the assets in the account. Sometimes this fee is a "trailer fee" paid by mutual fund companies and sometimes it is a management fee paid directly by the client. In this latter type of account, as the account grows, the remuneration grows as well because it is calculated as a percentage of the value of the account.

In theory, this fee-based type of account, sometimes called a *wrap account* because a bundle of services are all wrapped into one fee, is better for the client. It removes the incentive for the financial advisor to make unnecessary trades in the account. Since the client does not pay commissions on trades, he or she does not need to be concerned that a recommendation is being made simply to generate revenue for the financial advisor. In a fee account—where the advisor's fee grows with the growth of the account—the advisor's incentive is to have a larger account. Both you and your advisor benefit as the account grows.

One risk of a fee-based account, however, is that it may encourage the advisor to take unnecessary risks with your money. A higher return means the portfolio will grow faster and generate a higher amount in fees. If the higher-risk strategy fails, the advisor will lose a small amount of fee income, but you may lose your financial security.

Another industry bias to watch for is promotional material masquerading as information to educate the public. Assume that most of the brochures, newsletters, and advertisements coming out of the financial industry are guilty until proven innocent.

You have likely heard many times the following bit of advice: invest in the market and stay for the long term. It is generally good for the industry when investors stay in for the long term, but it is not always good for the investor, and herein lies another industry bias. For example, when investors take their money and buy treasury bills (the lowest-risk investment), few commissions are generated and the brokerage firm's profits are reduced. However, in a period when the stock markets are overvalued by many traditional indicators, common sense would suggest that very low-risk investments might indeed be the right investment for the average investor.

Brokerage firms and financial advisors are sometimes reluctant to recommend strategies that, while they might be good for the individual, would be disastrous if followed by the industry as a whole. The problem is that an individual may be able to protect himself in the event of a market crash by removing his money from the equity market. But if everyone removed their money, it would cause the very same market crash that they all want to avoid.

If the advisor moved all of his clients to cash because he feared a market crash, he would be out of business because, typically, no fees are generated on cash. When the advisor stops generating fees or commissions, he is literally out of business and his office is given to another advisor who is generating more commissions.

An example of biased advice is the illustration that is often presented in financial seminars showing how an investor's average return would be reduced if she missed the 20 best days in the market. This example is used to support the argument of not trying to time the market. Obviously, if you are out of the market during the best up days, your overall return will be significantly lower. But the other side of this argument is rarely discussed in these seminars. If an investor misses the 20 worst down days in the market, she would avoid losses—in fact, the difference is even greater. If you could choose being out of the market either for the 20 best up days or the 20 worst down days, you would be better off missing the worst down days.

BOTTOM LINE: Never forget that in the eyes of the financial industry you are a profit centre. Some of the industry's "educational advice" is conventional wisdom: for example, start saving at an early age. Yet other often-quoted advice, such as to stay in the market for the long term, may be more beneficial to the industry than to the individual investor.

WHAT YOU CAN DO NOW: Study impartial books, newsletters, and websites. These are written or sponsored by firms or individuals who are not trying to sell you something. Compare their viewpoints with the information supplied by industry sources.

Tip 18
Know How Your Financial Advisor Gets Paid

It may not happen often, but occasionally a financial advisor can be influenced by the different level of commissions that can be earned on different investment recommendations.

Most financial advisors are completely honest and go the extra mile to do what is best for their clients. Intelligent advisors know that their most important asset is their reputation for honesty and integrity. Enlightened self-interest is therefore enough to ensure that they will always do what is best for their clients and avoid any action that might hurt their reputation.

However, as in every industry, we do hear about financial advisors who, in order to generate fees, make recommendations for changes that are at best unnecessary and at worst may even be detrimental (after fees) to the client.

It is not always wrong when an investment advisor recommends the investment that pays the higher commission. Sometimes a change in the portfolio is necessary. For example, consider a situation in which for two investments all other things, such as potential return, potential risk, liquidity, tax efficiency, and correlation with the rest of the portfolio, are equal. An advisor can hardly be faulted for recommending the investment that pays the higher commission.

It is unlikely, however, that all other things will be completely equal. Financial advisors must therefore always be on their guard to ensure that their recommendations serve their clients' best interests.

Some compensation arrangements remove most of the potential for conflict of interest and other arrangements remove all such potential. It is worthwhile, therefore, for the client to understand the different types of compensation arrangements that are available.

The Financial Advisors Association of Canada (Advocis) describes the following four common types of compensation arrangements:

FEE ONLY:
The advisor is compensated through fees that are based on the time and complexity of the planning needs. Implementation of any recommendations may

be facilitated through the advisor but will be done by third parties who are licensed to sell the products being acquired. The advisor will not be compensated over and above the fees identified in the client–advisor agreement.

FEE PLUS COMMISSION:

The advisor is compensated through fees based on the time and complexity of the planning needs and will also receive compensation through commissions, finder's fees, and/or brokerage fees. These additional revenues will be received as a result of the purchase of investment, insurance, and other financial products as part of the implementation of the action plan.

FEE OFFSET:

The fees will be determined based on the time and complexity of the planning needs but will be reduced to reflect any commissions or referral fees received for transactions undertaken as a part of the implementation of the action plan. More specifically, the advisor will calculate how much annual fee revenue is required to implement the planning needs and to provide ongoing, continuous service, and deduct from this amount the estimated annual compensation expected in the form of commissions or referral fees, in order to arrive at a net amount payable annually.

COMMISSION ONLY:

The advisor is compensated through commissions, finder's fees, and/or brokerage fees. These revenues will be received as a result of the purchase of investments, insurance, and other financial products as a part of the implementation of the action plan.

Another type of compensation arrangement that exists within the brokerage industry is the managed account arrangement. In this case, no commissions are charged on trades within the account. Instead, an annual fee (usually between 0.75% and 1.5%) is charged on the assets in the account.

BOTTOM LINE: Even if it is only to put your mind at ease and to satisfy yourself that your advisor always has your best interests at heart, you must understand completely how your advisor is compensated.

WHAT YOU CAN DO NOW: If you are not certain as to how your financial advisor is being compensated, ask for clarification.

Part 3
Mastering the Market Basics

"How can institutional investors hope to outperform
the market . . . when, in effect, they are the market?"

Charles D. Ellis,
author and Wall Street authority

Tip 19

Be Realistic about the Nature of the Market

It is never wise to base your financial future on false hope. Average investors can't expect to beat the market consistently unless they take on additional risk. And they usually wind up with greater losses than they imagined.

When setting your objectives for investing in the stock market, you have a choice between old school thinking and new school thinking.

The old school way is to try to beat the market. If the stock market goes up by 10%, you expect your portfolio to go up by 12% or more. If the stock market falls in value, you expect your portfolio to fall by a smaller percentage than the market as a whole. If the market drops by 30%, and your portfolio drops by only 25%, you have still beaten the market.

If you are into the old school mode of thinking, you will have some level of satisfaction as long as you do, in fact, beat the market.

New school thinking, however, recognizes that most investors can't beat the market. All investors together make up the market. If everyone could beat the market, it would be like everyone in a high school math class performing above the class average.

There will be some investors who outperform the average in any given year, but they are likely to be found in the ranks of financial institutions, and the trading departments of banks and brokerage firms. These institutions, which trade for their own accounts, have the resources, infrastructure, experience, information, and ability to trade in all markets around the world on a 24-hour basis. These are the institutions that the average investor is trading against. For every buyer or seller who makes a bad choice, there is always another buyer or seller on the other side of the trade who, with better information, was able to make a better choice.

Fortunately, in the long run, you don't have to beat the market to benefit from stock market growth, you only have to do as well as the stock market average. And, for most investors, having a portion of their investment portfolio "in the market" during the past century has proved to be a wise investment, even when they only did as well as the market average.

While it is almost impossible to outperform the market consistently unless you are willing to take on higher risk, it is very easy to consistently perform as well as the market. The easy way to ensure that you do as well as the market is to purchase index funds or the index itself through exchange-traded funds (ETFs). These are investments that have low fees and generally have the same return as the stock market as a whole. (For more on ETFs, see pages 192–194.)

When you invest in individual stocks or equity mutual funds, you are, in effect, trying to beat the market. There is no other practical financial reason to own individual stocks, as opposed to an index fund or ETF, other than the hope that you can outperform the market as a whole.

There is another reason, however, to own individual stocks. Just as some individuals enjoy winning at the racetrack or winning at the blackjack table, some investors enjoy the thrill of opening the newspaper to see how their stocks are doing. It is perfectly sensible to invest in individual stocks if you are doing so for the fun of it, as long as you don't also think you're going to beat the market in the process.

Trading in individual stocks or regular mutual funds incurs trading costs and income tax costs. These two additional costs add to the difficulty of beating the market. A smarter approach, used by pension and endowment funds, is to invest a significant portion of the portfolio in exchange-traded funds or index mutual funds, thereby benefiting from lower fees and increased income tax efficiency.

Mutual funds are not the answer to consistently beating the market without taking additional risk. Mutual funds are ranked by their quartile performance. The understandable objective of every mutual fund manager is to be above average—to rank in the first or second quartile in terms of performance. But, according to the law of averages, only half will be above average while the other half will be below average, ranking in the third and fourth quartile. Management fees are an additional cost that makes it difficult for mutual funds to beat the market. You may want to rethink your strategy, therefore, if you own equity mutual funds that have high management fees.

Without question, some mutual fund managers do outperform the market. In trying to find these superior managers, the average investor faces two problems. The first is to determine whether the recent performance was due to skill or luck. The second is to know how much additional risk was taken to get this result. And don't forget that last year's top-quartile manager is rarely still in the top quartile by the time two or three years have passed.

Compromise is often the best approach. One route to follow is the "core and explore" approach. In this strategy, ETFs or index funds are used for the core of the equity investments. The core investment portion is supplemented by using active managers (those who try to beat the market) to explore opportunities for enhanced returns in market areas where their specialized knowledge may give them a shot at earning an incremental return.

The number of investors using ETFs is growing every year. However, this form of investment is not popular and is rarely recommended by brokerage firms or individual financial advisors. One reason that ETFs are not popular is that these investments do not pay trailer fees to advisors. Another reason is that most financial advisors sincerely believe that they will be able to beat the market consistently.

BOTTOM LINE: Don't waste your time trying to pick stocks or mutual funds that are going to beat the market. Use a low-cost index fund or an exchange-traded fund for the bulk of your equity exposure.

WHAT YOU CAN DO NOW: Make sure that your financial plan is based on realistic assumptions regarding the rate of return you expect. Don't expect that your mutual funds are going to produce a higher return than the market itself unless higher risk is taken.

Tip 20

Understand How Emotion and Logic Move the Market

If you think the market moves on logic, you may try to use logic to predict the market's direction over the short term. The truth is that the market moves on emotion. If you think it moves on logic and fundamentals, you are likely going to lose money.

It is easy to think that the market moves based on logic, facts, or events that occur in the world. We see the changes in the markets, we know the facts about certain events, and then we mentally create a cause-and-effect relationship. However, it is group thinking or the herd mentality, not facts, that cause major shifts in the market. Believing that the market moves mainly on facts can cause you to multiply your investment losses. Consider what superstar investor Warren Buffett has said: "When the price of a stock can be influenced by a 'herd' on Wall Street with prices set at the margin by the most emotional person, or the greediest person, or the most depressed person, it is hard to argue that the market always prices rationally. In fact, market prices are frequently nonsensical."

When the herd believes the market is going up, we decide to invest. When the market starts to go down, many of us fear the worst and decide to sell. This emotional response often outweighs the logic of sticking with the investment strategy.

Financial results are based on facts. What influences the market, however, are not those facts, but how the facts are interpreted. Even more important is how the actual financial results compare with the results that the investment community expected.

Markets change direction at the top of a bull market because most people who want to invest already have jumped on the bandwagon and are in the market. With no new supply of investors, the market falls from lack of available buyers to pick up the shares of those people who need to sell for any of a number of reasons.

At the bottom of a bear market, the market starts to turn around because most of those people fearful of losing more money have already sold their shares. With no ready supply of cheap shares, the market starts to rise because, with the sellers already out of the market, the buyers have to buy shares from those who are less willing to sell.

As Robert Prechter, who writes *The Elliott Wave Theorist* newsletter, points out, there is utilitarian economics, and there is herd-mentality economics. We can use televisions as an example. In utilitarian economics, as the price of TVs goes higher, the demand for TVs will fall; as their price drops significantly, the demand will increase. When the price is very high, people will delay making a purchase, and when the price is very low, consumers may buy a TV for every room in the house. This is a reasonable and logical way to manage one's money.

On the other hand, when buying stocks on the stock market, people use a very different logic. When buying stocks, the demand increases as the price goes higher and the demand drops as the price falls. This is exactly the opposite of what logic would dictate. The higher the price for individual stocks, the more stock investors want to buy, and as the price drops, investors have less and less desire to buy. In fact, they usually want to sell what they already own.

It is as if people were thinking, "The herd is running in this direction so this must be the right way to go." Individually, they don't know which way to go or why the herd is running in that direction but assume that someone else does know. They don't want to be left out, so they follow the herd because it seems safer.

At the end of a cycle, at the critical point where the main trend of the market changes, either to a bull market or a bear market, most investors will assume, wrongly, that the market will continue on its previous course. The average investor and the majority of experts will be equally wrong and their advice will compound the problems for those following their advice.

Unfortunately, investment managers also find it safest to run with the herd. If a manager loses money in a year when most other managers also lose money, he is unlikely to be fired. However, if he moves out of the market but the crash he fears does not occur, he is likely to be fired for underperforming at a time when most managers had a very good year. In cases like this, the manager often decides to stick with the herd even though his common sense and instincts tell him to stand aside.

BOTTOM LINE: Investors would be better off not listening to experts who predict which way the market will go. If you are going to listen to the experts, however, take the contrarian approach: try to determine what the consensus is and then bet that the opposite will happen.

WHAT YOU CAN DO NOW: Stop trying to use logic to predict where the market will go. Instead, focus on saving money and sticking to your investment strategy whether the market is rising or falling.

Tip 21

Don't Try to Predict the Impact of World Events on the Market

Overconfidence is one of the greatest dangers to both the professional and the average investor. Overconfident investors tend to take more risks until they eventually suffer a huge loss.

There are only a few types of major events where we can confidently predict their impact on the stock market. For example, another major terrorist attack in North America would almost certainly result in the markets going lower. Also, a natural disaster such as an earthquake in California would cause the markets to fall. For the most part, however, it is futile to forecast the reaction of the market to major happenings, or to base buy and sell decisions on predicting how the market will react to any event.

Predicting the impact of events on the market would be easy—if we lived on a small island with only a few companies, few products, and no access to products from outside the island. In addition, everyone on the island would have to receive the same news at the same time and respond the same way.

In reality, the market is influenced by so many factors that the news in the paper is a relatively poor guide to what is actually happening. This information is rarely accurate enough or timely enough to guide you to profitable trading decisions.

Competent investment managers, with all their experience, resources, and capital, find it difficult to anticipate the market's reaction to world events. How can the individual investor hope to do better? Even professional managers who run large hedge funds often lose money on more than half of their trades. (They usually still make money overall because they quickly sell their losers and they let their winners ride.)

The large international banks and hedge funds have developed the most sophisticated computer modelling programs in the world but still have difficulty in predicting the timing, extent, and degree to which certain events will affect the major stock markets of the world.

BOTTOM LINE: Don't try to beat the market by being overconfident of your knowledge or insight. You'd do as well by flipping a coin. If you want to benefit from the performance of the market, the easiest way is to buy the market by way of an ETF or an index fund.

WHAT YOU CAN DO NOW: Stop trying to anticipate short-term movements of the market.

Don't Fall for End-of-the-Day Explanations of Market Action

Thinking that the market can be explained so easily leads investors to think that they will be able to predict how the market will react to other events.

As Warren Buffett, the second-richest man in America, has put it, "We've long felt that the only value of stock forecasters is to make fortune tellers look good." The problem with oversimplifying the market is that it breeds overconfidence, and overconfidence leads to mistakes and investment losses.

If you read the papers or listen to business news channels, you will always get an explanation as to why the stock market went up or down that day. These explanations have little value for long-term investing. For the most part, these commentators are making up a plausible story, one that seems to be a reasonable explanation based on what actually happened.

An analogy might be found in the sports pages where the reporter is trying to explain why the winner of two almost equally matched football teams won yesterday's game. In reality, a great many factors had an impact on the game. These factors might include coaching expertise, the level of conditioning of each of the players, each team member's motivation and desire to win, the strategy adopted by the coach, the number of times the strategy was practised, not to mention luck, wind conditions, and temperature. There could be many other things, including the fact that one of the key defence players was experiencing some personal problems affecting his sleep and concentration.

Most of these factors will be unknown to the reporter covering the game, while one thing stands out to all spectators: that the star quarterback on team "A" was having a great game and his efforts motivated his team to new heights. The reporter writes that the game was won because of this player's outstanding performance. The true explanation, besides all the factors listed above, might be that the opponent assigned to guard the quarterback was playing poorly, making the star shine more brightly.

Based on the report of this sportscaster, fans might think that the key to predicting performance is whether or not the star quarterback is playing.

In fact, if fans really knew all of the factors involved, they might do better at predicting the winner by finding out how well the defence slept the night before.

Many explanations oversimplify the outcome and give the impression that cause and effect can be determined. In reality, there usually are too many unknowns. At best, a 30-second, end-of-the-day report on the stock market focuses attention on only one of an immense number of factors that influence the market on a given day. The real cause of market fluctuations cannot be so easily determined. It is not always possible to know how the market will react to the day's events, whether it is the outbreak of another war, a change in interest rates, or a rise in unemployment.

The following is an example of the folly of trying to interpret the meaning of the market's rise and fall. The stock market falls by 2% on the same day that a report is released saying that consumers are spending less. Referring to this consumer survey, the business news reporter says that the market fell as a result of investors' fears that corporate profits will be lower.

The reporter is suggesting a direct and simple causal relationship where none really exists. We are expected to believe that investors, collectively, (a) were aware of the report, (b) understood it, (c) feared that lower spending would lead to lower profits and therefore a loss of jobs, and (d) decided that this would mean the market would be lower in the future. The reporter implies that investors decided, based on these factors, that they should sell today.

In fact, when the markets go up or down on a given day, the ultimate reason is the cumulative effect of decisions by millions of investors and investment managers. Most are not even aware of the event reported to be the cause of the rise or fall of the market that day.

Buyers and sellers are always equal. A share is never sold unless there is a buyer on the other side of the transaction. The speed of the up-and-down market depends on the eagerness of buyers or sellers. When the market falls, the sellers are more eager than the buyers. As a result, the sellers make the offer to sell more attractive by offering to sell at a lower price. When the market rises, buyers are more eager to buy than sellers are eager to sell. Buyers give the sellers a greater incentive by offering a higher price than was offered on the previous day.

A vast number of reasons can prompt this change, on either side, to buy or sell.

Most reasons for market fluctuations are entirely unrelated to the day's news events. For example, if the Canadian market goes up, it is more likely to be a result of what happens in the US markets or in currency markets, or to the liquidity needs of the selling public, than some specific local or national event.

There is a huge difference between having an informed opinion and being able to predict the movement of a particular stock, let alone predict the movement of the market as a whole.

The majority of opinion formers who appear on TV business programs should be looked upon not as prophets but as entertainers, promoters, or salespeople. The people invited on the shows to analyze the markets usually work in the financial markets. They are articulate and have clear opinions. These guests generally have careers and incomes at stake and they have their own biases. Most often, they want the bull market to continue. If the public gives up on stocks and stops watching TV channels that promote stocks, then the guests' jobs may be on the line. They have a huge incentive to encourage viewers to stay in the market.

One expert expresses opinions based on experience, prejudices, intelligence, education, peer groups, and facts, both known and unknown. Another expert with different world experiences interprets these same facts in the opposite way. Still another expert with the same facts but a different background comes up with a totally different solution on the six o'clock news.

Usually, the most convincing expert is the one most likely to be wrong. When evaluating experts, look for those who admit that they may be wrong.

BOTTOM LINE: The market moves based on the collective emotions of all its participants. Explanations as to why the market went up or down on a particular day should be taken with a grain of salt. If you are going to watch business news, the safest approach is to assume that the people who are explaining the market's fluctuations are simply making it up as they go along.

WHAT YOU CAN DO NOW: Ignore the end-of-the-day explanations of the business news analyst. Make your investment decisions based on a financial plan that tells you the rate of return you need to earn and build/create a diversified portfolio designed to earn this rate of return over the long term.

Don't Try to Get a Higher Yield without Higher Risk

A sophisticated investor may decide to take a specific type of risk in order to try to get a higher rate of return, but knows what additional risk he is taking on. The casual investor tries to get a higher return but does not realize that extra risk is involved, whether it be risks related to events, liquidity, defaults, or interest rates.

It is generally safe, when looking at individual investments within the same asset class, to assume that higher return means higher risk. Corporate bonds are a good example. If one corporate bond is offering a higher rate of return, it may mean there is greater risk of default—that the issuing company is unable to repay the principal when the bond matures. It may mean higher liquidity risk—that there may not be a market to sell the bond before it matures. Or it may mean greater interest rate risk—a greater chance that rising interest rates or inflation will reduce the value of the bond between now and maturity. (See Part 5 for a description of the different types of risk.)

It is almost always a waste of time to look for a bond with a higher yield unless you are prepared for higher risk. To understand the logic, it is essential to have an understanding of the bond market. Using the corporate bond market as an example, the reason that you can only get a higher yield if you take higher risk is due to the efficiency and the size of this bond market.

Thousands of companies issue bonds and the number of buyers is even higher. Among these buyers are professionals whose sole focus is evaluating the creditworthiness of corporate bond issues. These specialists have powerful analytical tools, years of experience and, sometimes, inside information about potential risks of default. They also have good insights about the economy and the likely direction of interest rates.

Furthermore, bond specialists have, or should have, broad knowledge of comparable issues. If a company wants to sell a new bond issue in the corporate bond market, the professionals will know how this offering compares, both in price and risk, with the hundreds of other issues available on the market.

Based on their experience, bond specialists usually make accurate evaluations of the risk inherent in a particular issue. If a particular bond is paying a higher than average rate of return, it is not because it was overlooked by the hundreds of other professionals who could have purchased it before you did. The yield is higher because these hundreds of other professionals refused to buy the bond when it was offered at a lower yield. Given the risk involved, the bond professionals decided that other comparable corporate bond issues offered a better return for the same risk. To sell the bond, the bond sellers had to adjust the price so that the yield is high enough to attract buyers and offset the risk seen by the bond traders.

It makes no sense, therefore, to ask your financial advisor to shop around for the best rate of return, hoping to get a higher return without taking additional risk. A retail bond investor may not understand this risk-and-return rule. But the fact remains: the bond issue that yields a higher return does so because the risk of loss is also higher. The risk may have to do with defaults, interest rates, or liquidity. Or perhaps there is a risk of a downgrade. In any case, you can be sure that if a higher return is offered, there is some risk that is significantly higher.

While efficient, the bond market is not perfect. Pricing inefficiencies do occur from time to time. These inefficiencies, however, can be taken advantage of most effectively by those who specialize in the bond market, such as managers of fixed-income arbitrage hedge funds. Using sophisticated computer-generated models, these managers invest millions in each transaction and therefore incur very low fees. The professionals also buy direct from the company rather than on a retail basis.

Given a retail bond investor's limited resources, he is highly unlikely, no matter how much shopping around he does, to come up with a bond with a higher yield but no higher risk. This is not to say that the investor should never go for the higher return. He should just do so with his eyes open.

BOTTOM LINE: You may not understand the nature of the additional risk you are taking, but if you are expecting to earn a yield that is higher than the yield of government bonds, you are definitely taking on some additional risk—risk that bond traders recognize.

WHAT YOU CAN DO NOW: Prepare a financial plan or refine your current plan to show what rate of return you need to earn to achieve your goals. Have your financial advisor create an investment portfolio that can be expected to earn that return with the least possible risk.

Tip 24

Never Assume That a Good Product Means a Higher Share Price

When you buy a stock primarily because you like the product, you are giving too much weight to only one of many variables that will affect the price of the stock.

Sometimes investors hear about what is described as a marvellous new consumer product. They make sure to note the company's name and find out more about it on the Internet, and from other sources.

The product and the company appear to be sure winners. The investor gets excited and decides to buy the stock. The reality, however, is that while the stock may go higher, it is just as likely to drop in value. Having an excellent product is only one, and not even the most important, of the factors affecting the price of the stock. Only a company with an absolute monopoly is a sure shot to succeed with a great product.

Perhaps the company's excellent potential is already priced into the stock. Let's assume that a company is expected to grow by a factor of 10 over the next two years. It earns 10 cents a share now and therefore in two years it is expected to earn $1 per share. Assume that the stock is now trading at $30 per share. If the expected growth does occur, and this is not a sure bet, the stock will still be overpriced in two years' time, because you would be paying $30 for a stock that still is earning only $1 per share. That makes for a very high price–earnings ratio at 30 to 1. During the past 100 years, a price–earnings ratio of about 15 is normal. Historically, when the price-earnings multiple hit 25, it was the signal that the share price might fall.

Of course, in the short term, a positive spin on the story of the stock can influence the stock price and it may go higher. If the public perceives the stock as being hot, the demand may be so great that the stock, for a time, will sell well above its true value. Then again, if investors lose faith in the company, they may dump the stock and force the price even lower than its true value. In both situations, the stock is moving on hype and emotion, not on the strength of the product line.

Having a good product is not enough. Management has to show that it can run the company so successfully that the share price will rise.

Professionals know that a stock's price is also greatly influenced by the price and performance of the company's competitors.

Buying shares in an individual company is, in effect, trying to beat the market, a mug's game, as I have emphasized. If your objective is to have some fun and test your skills against the market's participants, then by all means go for it. Just don't make this the core of your investment strategy.

BOTTOM LINE: Having a great product may be a good first step for a company, but this in no way ensures that the company's stock price will go higher, particularly if it is already overpriced by traditional valuation measurements.

WHAT YOU CAN DO NOW: Focus on your overall investment strategy, not on individual stocks that you think will beat the market.

Tip 25

Recognize That You Can Make Money in a Bear Market

Investors who think that everyone loses in a bear market may lose more capital than necessary because they become more accepting of losses.

Some investors believe that when the market goes down, everyone loses money. In fact, when skilled investment managers believe that the market is going to go lower, they can position themselves to make as much money (if they are right and the market does go lower) as they can make when they position themselves for a rising market and the market obliges by going higher.

The key is to understand the difference between being "long" the market and being "short" the market. Being long a stock is simply another way of saying you own a stock. Being short a stock means that you borrowed a stock and then sold it and now you have the obligation to return the stock when you are asked to do so.

As an example of a short sale, imagine that when Nortel was trading at $100 per share you believed it was due to go lower and you called up your financial advisor and told her to make a short sale of 100 shares of Nortel. Your financial advisor arranged this sale by having her firm lend you 100 shares of Nortel, which you then sold at the market price of $100 per share. The proceeds from this sale were $10,000 and this money was deposited to your account. At some point, you know you will have to purchase 100 shares of Nortel on the open market so that you can return the 100 shares to the brokerage firm. If you repurchased the shares when they were trading at $10 per share, then you would have made a profit, before trading costs, of $9,000.

There are significant risks to selling short because after you borrow the shares and sell them, the shares may go up in value rather than down in value as you expected. In the above example, if the price of Nortel shares went up to $150 after you sold them at $100, then you would have to buy on the open market to replace the shares you borrowed from your broker and you would suffer a loss of $5,000, plus your trading costs.

Selling short is a risky proposition for the average investor, but in the hands of an experienced money manager it is an effective tool to reduce losses in a bear market. Investors must understand that with short selling their potential for loss is almost unlimited, whereas with a "long" position, they cannot lose more than 100% of their investment.

One of the most significant differences between hedge funds and mutual funds is that hedge funds are permitted to sell short while mutual funds are not. Since mutual fund managers are not permitted to use this risk-reducing tool, some industry experts describe mutual fund managers as working with one hand tied behind their back.

True diversification means holding different asset classes selected so that the gains on one type of security can be expected to offset the losses on other asset classes. In a bear market there is no better way to minimize the loss to the portfolio as a whole than to have asset classes that have some short exposure to the market. The profit of these short positions may go a long way toward offsetting the losses on the long positions.

BOTTOM LINE: Selling short is a very risky strategy for investors to undertake on their own. However, owning a professionally managed investment that has some short exposure can reduce losses in a bear market.

WHAT YOU CAN DO NOW: Ask your advisor about investment products, such as hedge funds, that have some short exposure to the market.

Tip 26

Know When Enough Research Is Enough

Trying to get all available information delays the decision to buy or sell and lulls you into thinking that more information will help you predict how this investment will perform.

Sometimes, individuals wisely avoid making investment decisions because they want to gather additional information. That's fine, but as computer scientist Peter Wyckoff has put it, "If you wait too long to buy, until every uncertainty is removed and every doubt is lifted at the bottom of a market cycle, you may keep on waiting, and waiting."

Information is undoubtedly valuable. But there comes a point where knowledge and critical judgment are needed. That extra bit of information will not always contribute to better investment decisions.

Sometimes, the stock market goes higher or lower simply because most people expect it to go in a certain direction. As people act on that belief, they create the pressure that causes the market to go in that direction. In these cases, more knowledge is of limited value because the market is moving on the emotion of the masses. Thus, the market moves on fear, greed, perceptions, and varying interpretations of facts, rather than on hard facts.

At the height of the dot-com craze, I had a discussion with my son, who has extensive knowledge of companies involved in Internet security and encryption. He knew the relative market share held by each of the major players and he knew when the patents on their encryption formulas expired. He had a good idea of the relative strengths of each encryption algorithm. I suggested that, with this type of knowledge, he could get a good job as an analyst with one of the brokerage firms. He pointed out that it was of little advantage at that time to know a lot about this particular industry and the business potential of these companies. Share prices were moving, based not on any logic or facts but on the whims of day traders who didn't know a thing about the fundamentals of the companies they were trading.

In such a market, having an understanding and knowledge of the companies could have been a disadvantage to my son. Fortunately, he realized that knowing the fundamental reason for the existence of these companies was not enough. Their shares were trading in a high volume but the buying and selling was based on emotion, not on logic.

Most investors decide to buy at times of great optimism and sell at times of great pessimism. Yet we know that some of the most successful investors in the world are "contrarians." They sell when others want to buy and buy when others want to sell.

Billionaire investor Sir John Templeton, creator of some of the world's largest and most successful international investment funds, attributes his success to "being generous." He willingly sells his shares when shares are in high demand by the public and he willingly buys shares when the public wants to unload them.

More information about a stock or market segment, or more information about the mood of investors as a whole, is not likely to help you beat the market. And if you can't beat the market, you should try simply to match the market. You can do this very easily by buying exchange-traded funds and index funds.

Just because you can never get enough information to guarantee a successful trade does not mean you should skip homework entirely. The areas where you should do your homework, however, are in selecting your financial advisor, working with the advisor to prepare and keep a financial plan updated, and monitoring investment performance.

Also, investors who delay making decisions—to do that extra research— might find the opportunity to buy or sell at a reasonable price has passed them by.

BOTTOM LINE: Do your homework—not to help you predict short-term market movements, but rather to become clear on your financial goals. Get and keep a financial plan up to date, and work with your advisor to get an investment portfolio designed to earn, on average, the rate of return you need to earn in order to achieve your financial goals.

WHAT YOU CAN DO NOW: Spend time to understand your overall investment strategy and why you expect it will work. Stop trying to get the information that you think will help you predict which way a particular stock is going to go. Stop thinking that more homework will enable you to consistently beat the market without taking greater-than-average risk.

Part 4

Measuring and Monitoring Risk

"You can't manage what you can't measure."

William Hewlett,
co-founder of Hewlett-Packard, which began in a small garage

Tip 27
Don't Risk Using a Risk-Tolerance Questionnaire

A risk-tolerance questionnaire assumes that you will act logically, rather than emotionally, when your investment portfolio is down by 20% and the industry experts are predicting that things will get worse before they get better. This is an incorrect assumption because most investors react emotionally in such situations.

Typically, when a new client opens an account with the local investment firm, one of the first things her advisor will ask her to do is to complete a risk-tolerance questionnaire. The advisor will explain that her answers will help him decide how much risk she should take. A high tolerance for risk would suggest an investment mix with both higher risk and higher return potential.

To understand why this approach is wrong, you have to understand what market risk means. *Risk* generally refers to the volatility of the investment. *Volatility* is the measure of how frequently and to what degree an investment rises and falls in value.

Risk can also be described as the range of expected returns during a month or a year. In North America, over the past century, the range of returns for the broad stock market index, on an annual basis, is between –44% and +55%. Risk for an investment portfolio made up of government bonds is lower, between –15% and +15%.

Assume the client's answers to the questionnaire indicate that she is comfortable with a high level of risk. She indicates that she is willing to accept this higher risk in order to earn a higher return. There are four reasons why this method of determining the level of risk tolerance is wrong.

- Asking questions about risk does not give an accurate estimate of the risk someone can really take. The perception of risk is an emotional, not a logical, response. When the market is going up, and the investor is filled with optimism about how the new relationship is going to work, she is likely to indicate a tolerance for risk that is too high. To get reliable answers, the questions have to be asked when her stock portfolio has just fallen by 30% and she fears losing her home if losses on her investments continue, and the experts are predicting that the downward trend is going to continue.

- Part of the problem is that financial advisors have been trained to believe that (1) stocks ultimately will give higher returns than bonds, and (2) the investor should always go for the highest return possible. The advisor assumes the right mix is the one containing the highest percentage in stocks that the investor can tolerate—before panicking and selling everything in a bad bear market. The broad stock market index can drop by over 40% in one year (it happened in 1931). If the advisor determines the client's portfolio can absorb a 40% decline, the advisor may recommend a mix of almost all stocks. Such a drop in the portfolio's value is more than most investors want to experience. It is at this point that she throws in the towel, calling her financial advisor and telling him to sell everything. She thereby locks in her losses and probably never ventures near the stock market again.

- Even if the client seems to have the emotional fortitude to withstand a lot of risk, taking on more risk than necessary only increases the probability of her losing her capital someday. Not taking on enough risk is equally a wrong approach: when a client takes on too little risk, her returns will be lower and she may not have enough to meet the goals of her financial plan.

- The level of risk should be determined only after deciding on the rate of return you need to earn to meet the objectives in your financial plan. Preparing a plan will tell you what rate of return you need to earn and therefore what level of risk you need to take. (See Part 2 for advice on working with a financial planner.)

BOTTOM LINE: A risk-tolerance questionnaire may help protect the brokerage firm and the financial advisor, but it is not the best way for you to determine the level of risk you should be taking in your investment portfolio. A wise investor takes no more risk than is necessary to achieve his or her financial goals.

WHAT YOU CAN DO NOW: Prepare a financial plan that shows the rate of return you need. Have your financial advisor recommend an investment portfolio that can be expected to earn this rate of return with the least amount of risk possible. Find out how this portfolio should perform both in good and bad markets. Understand why the strategy is expected to work under those conditions.

Tip 28

Understand Both Types of Stock Market Risk

There are two types of stock market risk and there is no need to be exposed to both. It makes no sense to be exposed to non-systematic risk when it can be avoided so easily. Not understanding how to eliminate non-systematic risk creates exposure to more risk than necessary.

There are two types of stock market risk. One is very easy to avoid while the other is unavoidable if you invest in stocks. The first is the risk that the stocks you own will fall in value because the entire market falls. This is called systematic risk or market risk. The industry also calls it Beta risk.

This type of risk (loss) occurs in a bear market when the majority of stocks fall in value. Almost all stocks are likely to drop in a bear market, just as all ships at dock will drop lower at low tide. When the tide comes in (the next bull market), it lifts all ships.

It is not possible to eliminate systematic or Beta risk. The stock market is unpredictable. Yet, the impact of systematic risk can be reduced by diversifying your portfolio to include assets other than stocks, assets that are likely to rise in value as the stocks fall.

For example, a portfolio of stocks, bonds, cash, income trusts, and hedge funds will have lower volatility than one entirely made up of stocks. It is unlikely that all of the securities in the diversified portfolio will rise or fall in unison. If part of the portfolio is rising in value as another part is falling, the overall movement of the portfolio is reduced.

The second type of risk is non-systematic. You are affected by this risk when your stocks go down even though the market as a whole is on the rise. Obviously, your stock is underperforming the market.

A company's stock might not be doing well for any number of reasons, among them negative earnings surprises, disapproving comments from the auditor, firing of key personnel, loss of market share to the competition, fraud, or cash-flow problems. This can happen even though the market as a whole is going higher.

The good news is that non-systematic risk can be avoided. Buying your stocks through a mutual fund, or buying an exchange-traded fund, can greatly reduce non-systematic risk. You can also significantly reduce it if you diversify by purchasing at least 30 stocks. Studies have shown that owning 30 stocks is enough to eliminate 90% of non-systematic risk.

With only one or two stocks, you have a high-risk portfolio. If one of the stocks falls, your portfolio may drop significantly in value. With 30 or more stocks, the loss from one stock will normally be offset by a gain from another, leaving you only with the risk that the market as a whole (systematic risk) will fall in value.

A widely diversified portfolio is unlikely to become worthless even in a severe bear market. Losing everything should be a concern only if you own a single stock. In the absolutely worst-case scenario, based on the record of the past century, a stock portfolio could shrink by as much as 50%. But it is hard to imagine a greater loss, unless the entire financial system as we know it ceases to exist.

Although fortunes have been made by having a heavy concentration in a single stock, having "all your eggs in one basket" is not the wisest move for most investors. Those most likely to be investors in only one stock are long-time employees who have acquired stock in the company where they work. For reasons of loyalty or dedication to the company, they sometimes keep their portfolio in this single source. The much safer approach would be to have no more than 10% of assets in one investment, no matter how much you like a particular stock.

I have a close friend who was once a multi-millionaire (on paper). Some 90% of his net worth was tied up in the shares of the company he worked with. For reasons of loyalty, he felt he could not sell these shares, even though he was advised to diversify. The stock has now dropped in value by more than 90%. His retirement plans have changed dramatically.

BOTTOM LINE: For the average investor, it makes no sense to bear both systematic and non-systematic risk. You can't avoid Beta or systematic risk, but non-systematic risk can be significantly reduced either by purchasing index funds or exchange-traded funds, or by purchasing at least 30 stocks to diversify your portfolio.

WHAT YOU CAN DO NOW: Talk to your financial advisor about the wisdom of eliminating non-systematic risk from your portfolio.

Don't Ignore the History of the Asset Class

The real risk is described by the asset class. If you focus instead on a few years of a specific manager's investment performance, you are likely to underestimate the risk involved in any particular mutual fund.

Is past performance a good guide to future performance? Should you know the history or does history not matter because it is a poor indicator of the future?

As investors, it seems that we are always being told that past performance cannot be used as a predictor of future performance. Despite this disclaimer, mutual fund companies, in their advertisements, emphasize the historical rates of return of their best-performing funds. They do not disclose the performance of their worst-performing funds except where it has to be reported. And after three to five years of consistently bad performance, these funds are usually wound up or amalgamated with funds that have a better record.

If you ask your financial advisor about a stock that your neighbour says is a hot pick, the advisor likely will respond by telling you that the past record is no sure guide to future results. On the other hand, when your advisor calls to suggest buying a new managed investment, he likely will include in his recommendation a reference to past performance and the record of the investment manager.

As a measure of what will happen, the record of a stock is certainly not an infallible guide; it is, however, one of the best available guides.

None of us can predict what will happen in this century. Considering the past, however, we can easily imagine that the stock market will react based on emotion, just as it did during the last century. This gives us a good idea of what we can expect in the future during periods of both optimism and pessimism. So past performance is our best guide to future performance.

The problem is that past-performance information needs to be used correctly. Consider these points:

- When looking at the record of a mutual fund, the first factor to consider is the performance of the specific asset class. For example, if you are buying a Canadian equity mutual fund, you should focus on the performance of Canadian equities in general, not just the performance of the particular Canadian equity manager who manages this mutual fund. The risk, or volatility, of the asset class provides the best prediction of the performance the manager might achieve. If the stock market is going up, most Canadian equity managers will have a good year. If the market is going down, most managers are going to lose money that year.

- What you should look for is not the actual return in a single year, the average return over a number of years, or even the average return during the career of a particular manager. Rather, you should focus on the range of returns of the asset class during the relevant time period. For example, we know that the S&P 500 Index—one of the best measures of the stock market as a whole—has, over the past 100 years, moved in the range from −44% to +54%. This range describes the nature of this index: in the past, it has moved in a 100-point-or-so range and will likely do the same in the future. The history of the asset class gives you a reasonable expectation both for the expected return and for the degree of volatility in common stocks. The past record is quite reliable as a guide to understanding the range of expected returns for a specific type of investment.

- When looking at past performance, investors often make decisions using the wrong time periods. For example, when we look at a 10-year average return and a 10-year average volatility range, we may get a comfortable feeling about the level of risk over a 10-year period. This information is irrelevant, however, if the volatility of the investment over a one-year period is more than we can live with. To get to the 10-year return and 10-year volatility levels, we have to go through 10 single years, and it is during the higher volatility of the shorter periods that most investors become emotional and make the wrong decision, either to buy or sell.

BOTTOM LINE: Past performance, viewed correctly, can be very useful in predicting the average return and the range of returns for an investment.

Investors who use past performance incorrectly, and who look at a short-term average return rather than the volatility of the asset class over the past 100 years, are more like to experience losses.

WHAT YOU CAN DO NOW: Knowing that the stock market can drop by over 40% in one year, you should assess your investment portfolio and decide if you are comfortable with the risk.

Tip 30
Avoid Investments You Don't Understand

Making a purchase without understanding the nature of the investment can lead to unforeseen risks.

Most investors use some form of "structured" products, such as mutual funds, income trusts, hedge funds, or exchange-traded funds, in their portfolios. Individual stocks and bonds now make up only a small part of the investment opportunities available to investors.

Just as cars and computers have been vastly improved over recent decades, we now have many better, safer, and more complicated investment options. Yet, for every new product that offers the potential for a greater return with less risk, a copycat product is also available. It may seem to have many of the original's best features but it may have hidden fees and unexplained risks.

Mark Twain, in his short story "The $30,000 Bequest," was of the opinion that the best way to make money from stocks is to sell investment advice. That opinion could be updated today to say that the best way to make money in the investing world is to create and sell new investment products. Today, some of the brightest minds are busy creating new investment products or taking old investing ideas and updating them to take advantage of new technology and new global investing opportunities.

Most ordinary investors are busy people. They don't have the time to study stocks and bonds or the intricacies of the markets—not to mention understand income trusts, covered call programs, hedge funds, and structured notes with capital guarantees. Financial advisors themselves often struggle to grasp the complexities and risks of these new structured products. If we have a major downturn, a lot of advisors will be shocked to discover how these often misunderstood risks actually manifest themselves.

For example, look back to the 1980s when portfolio insurance was in vogue. This strategy was expected to protect clients in a falling stock market. When the crash came in 1987, we discovered that portfolio insurance, while great in theory, just did not work when the market went into free fall and everyone tried to cash in on the "insurance."

For the next 15 years, portfolio insurance was seldom mentioned and the strategy was not widely recommended. In 2003, however, I became aware of another new product based on the same investing principle, only this time it was not called portfolio insurance. This time it was simply referred to as a "leveraging and deleveraging strategy." The value of this product will not be evident until the next serious bear market takes hold.

It has always been a sensible strategy to avoid investing in things you don't understand. However, if you want to follow this rule, and you also want to enjoy good investment returns, you have to study some very complex investment products. For example, if you really want to understand hedge funds and certain structured investment products, you are going to have to make a serious commitment. Very few in the investment industry are specialists in hedge funds or even understand them. Knowledge has its rewards, however, and some of the more complicated investment strategies may offer higher returns without significantly higher risk.

Not everybody can be an expert. If you insist on a full understanding of every underlying strategy in, for example, a "fund of hedge funds," it is unlikely that you will ever buy this type of investment. This may be unfortunate because some of these investments have a history of providing an excellent return for the risk taken.

If you want to enjoy the benefits of many different types of structured products, such as hedge funds, you will probably have to rely on someone else's expertise. In these cases it may be that the best use of your time is to evaluate the expertise of your advisor and form an opinion as to whether she really understands the products she recommends. You should be aware of the advisor's experience, qualifications, and reputation. For example, if you are considering hedge funds, check out whether your advisor has acquired a certified hedge fund specialist (CHFS) or chartered alternative investment analyst (CAIA) designation.

If you are doing your own due diligence on an investment instrument, you should take the following steps:

- Look for proven track records. Understand that there is a difference between a real track record and a pro forma track record. The latter is simply a hypothetical record or a reconstruction of how the investment would have performed if it had been available in the past.

- Find out all the costs, including the hidden ones.
- Don't put too much money in one basket even if the investment seems very safe.
- Remember that, all things being equal, a solid guarantee from a major bank is a good thing.
- Don't be in a rush. If it is a good product, wait a few months and the people who created it will create another product.

When in doubt, stick with the structured products of firms that have been in business for decades and have billions of dollars under management. These firms might not put up the huge rate of return numbers that a small firm can generate over a short time, but these firms will likely have more experience, more risk controls, and a stronger guarantee.

BOTTOM LINE: You have a tough choice. You can limit your investments to what you currently know or you can take the time to study new structured products such as hedge funds. Or you can make certain that your financial advisor is sufficiently experienced and well enough qualified that you can safely accept her recommendations.

WHAT YOU CAN DO NOW: Because you don't want to miss out on excellent investment opportunities, you have to make a realistic assessment of your financial advisor's level of knowledge of new investment products.

Tip 31
Use the Sharpe Ratio

Unless you use the Sharpe Ratio, you are likely to fall into the trap of comparing returns rather than comparing risk-adjusted returns.

You don't have to know how to calculate the Sharpe Ratio, but you should know how it can help you choose better investments. The ratio takes its name from its inventor, William Sharpe, a finance professor at the prestigious Stanford University. All you really need to know is that the higher the ratio the better it is for the investor. A Sharpe Ratio of 0 or less is not very good. A Sharpe Ratio of 0 to 1 means that you are getting a fair return for the risk you are taking. A Sharpe Ratio higher than 1 is excellent.

The Sharpe Ratio allows you to compare dissimilar investments to determine which one gives the highest return for each "unit" of risk. For example, assume that you are trying to get the highest possible return for a given amount of risk and you are considering two investments. Investment A earned 7% and had a risk, or standard deviation, of 8% (standard deviation is the most common measure of risk). Investment B earned 9% and had a standard deviation of 20%.

Without knowing the Sharpe Ratio, it is difficult to know which investment offers the higher return per unit of risk. Obviously investment B had the better return, but did the higher return justify the higher risk?

If we do a calculation and find that the Sharpe Ratio of the first investment is 0.5, and that of the second investment is 0.3, then we know that the first investment is a better choice because it has the potential to give a higher return for each unit of risk.

Given a choice, and if all other things are equal, a person who buys the investment with the highest Sharpe Ratio will almost always make the right investment decision. The ratio can be worked out both for an individual investment and for your portfolio as a whole. Sharpe Ratios are readily available for mutual fund and hedge fund investments and if you have enough data, they can, with some difficulty, be calculated for individual stocks or bonds.

Perfectionists argue that the ratio is not the best guide because it is based on standard deviation, which measures the extremes both above and below the average return. For the purposes of the average investor, however, the Sharpe Ratio is the best guide for measuring risk and return.

As an investor, you have two pertinent questions for your advisor: "What is the Sharpe Ratio of this investment, and what is the Sharpe Ratio of my portfolio as a whole?"

For comparison, the average balanced mutual fund has a Sharpe Ratio of about 0.5. If your portfolio has a Sharpe Ratio of between 0.5 and 1 you are doing better than average. If it is less than 0, you've lost money during that period and you are taking more risk than necessary for the return you are expecting. As a general rule, investors will find the highest Sharpe Ratios in hedge fund investments.

BOTTOM LINE: In a perfect world, your financial advisor would tell you the Sharpe Ratio for any mutual fund investment that he recommends. When you use the ratio, you avoid the problem of comparing investments based only on return without taking risk into consideration.

WHAT YOU CAN DO NOW: Ask your financial advisor if he is able to calculate the Sharpe Ratio for your portfolio as a whole, as well as for any recommended mutual fund investment. Don't be disappointed if he cannot provide this number. Most advisors do not have the software tools to make this calculation.

Those who wish to make the calculation themselves can do so by taking the average monthly return and subtracting the "risk-free" rate of return, which is assumed to be the monthly rate for treasury bills. The remainder is then divided by the monthly standard deviation, which can easily be determined by using an Excel function. The result is then annualized.

Readers can find excellent examples of how to calculate a Sharpe Ratio by typing "Sharper Ratio" into any search engine.

Tip 32
Get a Second Opinion

Sometimes financial advisors lose their objectivity about their clients' portfolios. They may become defensive about their recommendations and fail to recognize an important mistake when it occurs. Without a professional second opinion, investors who are not knowledgeable about investing are at a disadvantage because they may not know what questions they should ask their advisors.

A close eye on health and finances is needed to enjoy happiness during your working life and your retirement. Our health is so important that we find it normal to ask for a second medical opinion before any major operation. In financial matters, however, it is less likely that an investor will seek out a second professional opinion. One reason for the reluctance is that many investors fear a second advisor will be unduly critical of a perfectly good portfolio because the second advisor, who is paid on commission, wants to try to win the account.

This reluctance is not entirely without justification. There will always be a few securities that have recently underperformed and these are often pointed to as evidence of bad strategy on the part of the other advisor. The implication is that the advisor who is reviewing the portfolio would never have made such a mistake.

Regrettably, in this competitive industry, where most financial advisors think they are smarter than their peers, you are likely to get pressure to move your account any time you visit a new financial advisor and ask for a second opinion.

There is a way you can get a second opinion without being exposed to sales pressure: by using the services of a third party such as a chartered accountant. You can ask the accountant to send out a "request for a second opinion letter" to three financial advisors. Your name is not revealed and the financial advisors are invited to respond to the accountant.

Investment advisors who receive this letter will be pleased to provide an independent analysis because they all want to develop and strengthen their relationships with accountants. You can be sure that the investment advisors will give their best analysis. Also, they may offer to discount their fees if given an opportunity to service your account.

When the CA receives the responses to the request for a second opinion, she forwards them to you. You then have three competitive quotes and three different opinions about how to construct a portfolio to meet your needs. The request for proposal form also asks the investment advisor to comment on the strengths and weaknesses of your existing asset mix. You are the winner when investment advisors compete for your business.

The key question to ask is, "Am I willing to spend a couple of hours and maybe the cost of a few hours of my CA's time in order to get three competitive quotes for my business?" Keep in mind that the cost of a poorly designed investment portfolio can quickly mount into thousands of dollars.

You can also try to get competitive quotes by sending out a request for a second opinion yourself; make sure, in the covering letter, to specify clearly that you will initiate any future contact.

BOTTOM LINE: It is worthwhile to get a second opinion on your investment portfolio. You can do this without subjecting yourself to unwanted sales pressure.

WHAT YOU CAN DO NOW: Consider using an unbiased source to get a second opinion on your investment portfolio. You can also consider having accounts with two different investment firms. That way you have an ongoing exposure to another investment approach and you may also increase your level of diversification. I can personally recommend going to my website *www.secondopinions.ca.*

Tip 33

Don't Obsess over Avoiding Stock Market Risk

The stock market represents an important asset class that most investors should hold. Investors who try to eliminate risk by avoiding stocks entirely may be exposing themselves to other risks that, in the long run, can be just as serious.

It really doesn't matter how the money disappeared, or where it went, if you don't have enough to maintain your lifestyle in retirement. The impact of a lower standard of living is the same whether your capital was eroded by inflation or deflation, or lost in a stock market crash. A wise and cautious investor therefore takes precautions against all risks.

The major risks you face include those related to inflation, deflation, currency fluctuations, reinvestment, interest rates, income tax, default, bad managers, liquidity, and fraud. But the biggest risk is running out of money after you stop working.

Some people invest only in bonds and bank-issued guaranteed investment certificates (GICs) because they hope to avoid all risk. However, they may lose if interest rates go higher, or if inflation rises, and they will pay more in income tax. They are also exposed to reinvestment risk. This is the risk that when the guaranteed investments mature, the capital may have to be reinvested at a lower rate. Retired people who became comfortable with a lifestyle based on earning 10% on GICs have had to make significant lifestyle adjustments when their matured funds had to be reinvested at 5%.

People buying real estate face the risk of deflation. And there are other factors to consider. Real estate generally falls in value when interest rates go higher. Furthermore, real estate markets can go up or down, and property is not a liquid investment.

Canadians who, in 2003, used their dollars to invest in US Treasury bills in the belief that this was a very safe investment came to understand the real meaning of currency risk as the US dollar fell against the Canadian dollar. Some very safe T-bill accounts lost almost 20% due to the increase in the value of the Canadian dollar versus the US dollar.

Sometimes, people invest in a managed portfolio of stocks to avoid non-systematic risk (see pages 80–81) only to incur "manager risk": the risk that occurs when the person managing your mutual fund makes a wrong call, resulting in your portfolio falling in value.

As already emphasized, a properly designed investment portfolio should be diversified to include many different asset classes. You want a number of asset classes to increase the probability that one or two of them will be rising in value to offset the loss in value of the asset classes that are in a down cycle. When losses are offset by gains, the overall risk of the portfolio is reduced.

Of course, if all of your capital is invested in the right asset class, at just the right time, you are going to be a big winner. If all your money happens to be in long-term bonds at a time when interest rates fall, your portfolio will increase in value sharply. However, don't plan on being this lucky.

For most investors, the safe and sensible approach is to diversify and not make large bets where success depends on any specific economic outcome.

BOTTOM LINE: There is safety in numbers—in this case, numbers of different asset classes. The best risk-reducing strategy is to be diversified by using multiple asset classes in your investment portfolio.

WHAT YOU CAN DO NOW: Check to see that you have at least three or four of the following asset classes in your investment portfolio: cash, short-term bonds, long-term bonds, common stocks (held as individual stocks, mutual funds, or ETFs), hedge funds, managed futures, and income trusts.

Tip 34

Don't Obsess over Short-Term Fluctuations

Focusing on short-term fluctuations may cause you to build a portfolio with very low fluctuation but with a return that will not be high enough to achieve your goal of financial independence.

The ups and downs of the market can be distracting. Investors often become so wrapped up in day-to-day fluctuations that they lose sight of the main objective: achieving their long-term financial goals. For most people, this objective can be simply expressed. They want enough money to keep up their standard of living (or perhaps even improve it), to retire when they want to, and to have financial independence until they die.

If your plan shows that you need an average return of 8% to achieve this objective, then you must keep this long-term average rate of return in sight. If you are in a properly diversified investment portfolio, you can ignore the daily or weekly changes in your portfolio's value.

Focusing totally on minimizing risk—which is easy if you also minimize return—could bring such a low return that you fail to meet your financial targets. This is like not seeing the forest for the trees. It is easy to avoid incurring loss by always investing in treasury bills. However, while this strategy will avoid market fluctuations, the low return on these investments could mean that you might not have as much as you need during your retirement.

To have financial independence in retirement, you must focus on the average rate of return needed over the long term. If the long-term rate of return requirement is higher than the very low return on treasury bills, then you have to accept fluctuation in order to get the higher return. This means there will be periods when you make money and periods when you lose money. With an all-stock portfolio, the value might be up by 40% or down by 40% in any one year. On the other hand, with a well-diversified portfolio, you will probably never make 40% but you also are unlikely to be down by more than 10% in any one year.

You can stop worrying about short-term changes in the value of your portfolio if you are confident that in the long run it will earn the return you need. That confidence comes from an understanding of historical returns of different asset classes and the historical performance range of a diversified portfolio during different time periods.

A well-designed portfolio also gives you the confidence to ignore downturns because (a) they should be quite small and (b) they will be anticipated and should be within the expected range of returns. Even in a well-diversified portfolio, there is always the possibility of the type of negative performance that happens only once every 20 years. When these events occur, even a perfectly designed portfolio can show a larger than expected loss. In a poorly diversified portfolio, however, losses should not be ignored—in fact, the first loss may only be a sign of worse losses to come.

If you have a portfolio that has just dropped in value by a greater amount than you thought possible, it is time to ask your advisor to clarify what is the expected range of returns over any one-year or one-month period.

BOTTOM LINE: If you have a suitably diversified portfolio, you should not trade away the long-term goal in order to avoid small fluctuations. If your portfolio has dropped in value by more than you expected, this may be an indication that it is not wisely diversified.

WHAT YOU CAN DO NOW: Ask your financial advisor to provide you with an estimate of the average return you can expect from your portfolio. Also ask for an estimate of how great a loss you should expect in the worst likely year.

Part 5

Controlling Risk

"Risk varies inversely with knowledge."

Irving Fisher,
in *The Theory of Interest* (1930)

Learn Why Negative Correlation Is a Positive Thing

If you don't understand negative correlation, and how it reduces risk, you may miss out on opportunities to increase returns while reducing risk at the same time.

Modern Portfolio Theory (MPT) provides an explanation of how you can reduce risk in an investment portfolio without also reducing the rate of return. MPT is a valuable tool. Harry Markowitz won the 1990 Nobel Prize in Economics for work done in 1952 in developing this theory.

Negative correlation is the key. Correlation is simply a measure of the degree to which investments typically move in the same or in the opposite direction. If you have two investments with negative correlation, one will be going up in value as the other is going down. If they are positively correlated, they will both be moving in the same direction, either up or down.

When your investments are negatively correlated, you can use higher-risk/higher-return investments in your portfolio and still reduce the overall risk. This is because the risk to the portfolio as a whole is reduced: when one higher-risk/higher-return investment is going down, another is typically going up in value to offset the decline.

Two investments are said to have perfect positive correlation when they not only go up at the same time but also do so by the same percentage. These investments would have a positive correlation of +1. Conversely, two investments have perfect negative correlation when one goes up and the other goes down by the same percentage. This correlation has a value of −1.

Two investments have zero correlation when the performance of one is generally unrelated to the performance of the other. In this case, knowing that the first investment has gone either up or down gives you no ability to predict which direction the second investment will take. The full range of correlation, from perfect positive to perfect negative, is from +1 to −1.

The S&P 500 Index is a commonly used benchmark for the stock market as a whole. Individual investments can be measured both in terms of how they are correlated with this index and how they are correlated with other investments.

Unfortunately, when investors are thinking of adding a new investment to their portfolio, they typically focus on the recent track record (the return) of the proposed addition. If it is good, that is usually seen as reason enough to add the investment. This is the wrong approach. A better criterion is to determine if it will reduce the risk of the portfolio. To answer that question, you have to ask your advisor how the potential investment is correlated with others you already have. If the new investment has negative or low correlation with the other investments in the portfolio, it will reduce the risk to the portfolio as a whole.

NEGATIVE CORRELATION REDUCES RISK

TWO INVESTMENTS POSITIVELY CORRELATED

	Investment A	Investment B	Combined Return A+B
Year 1	1%	6%	3.5%
Year 2	12%	13%	12.5%
Year 3	4%	7%	5.5%
Year 4	12%	16%	14%
Year 5	3%	6%	4.5%
Average Return	6.4%	9.6%	8%
Standard Deviation (Risk)	4.67%	4.13%	4.36%

Note: The combined portfolio's average return is 8% and the average risk (standard deviation) is 4.36%.

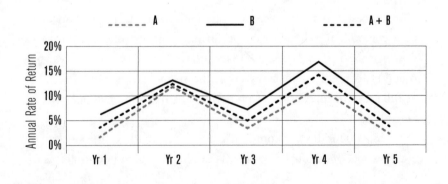

In the simplified illustration provided (see the charts and graphs on pages 100–101), you can see that the risk for the portfolio is reduced (2.29% versus 4.36%) when two investments with negative correlation are combined. The return for the portfolio is also higher (9.2% versus 8%), even though the risk is lower. In a portfolio made up of investments with negative correlation, the individual risks cancel each other out and the risk for the portfolio as a whole is lower.

TWO INVESTMENTS NEGATIVELY CORRELATED

	Investment A	Investment C	Combined Return A+C
Year 1	1%	12%	6.5%
Year 2	12%	2%	7%
Year 3	4%	18%	11%
Year 4	12%	6%	9%
Year 5	3%	22%	12.5%
Average Return	6.4%	12%	9.2%
Standard Deviation (Risk)	4.67%	7.38%	2.29%

Note: The combined portfolio's average return is 9.2% and the average risk (standard deviation) is 2.29%.

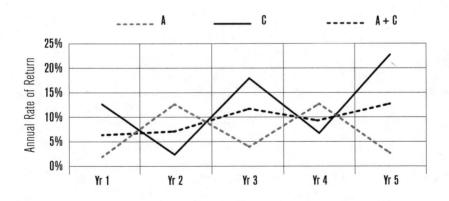

One of the most important things that we learn from Modern Portfolio Theory is that we should not be concerned about the performance of individual investments. We should focus on the risk and return of the portfolio as a whole.

BOTTOM LINE: Over the long term, and under normal circumstances, there are more effective ways to reduce risk from all sources than to move the portfolio to cash or treasury bills.

WHAT YOU CAN DO NOW: Ask your advisor how a proposed new investment is correlated with the rest of the investment portfolio.

Tip 36
Have Your Portfolio Optimized

If your investment portfolio is not optimized, you may be taking more risk than necessary for the rate of return you expect to earn.

In an optimized portfolio, the asset mix is designed to minimize risk for a certain level of return or to maximize return for a certain level of risk. Computer programs are available to help you achieve this desired mix. The computer selects investments to give the highest probability that a drop in value of one investment will be offset by an increase in value of another. (See Tip 35's discussion of negative correlation.)

Before computers, advisors relied on experience and guesswork to reduce overall portfolio risk. For example, an oil stock might be bought in combination with an airline stock, because a drop in the value of one was usually offset by a rise in the other. Here is another hypothetical example, used to explain how risk to the portfolio can be reduced. An investor might acquire shares in a factory that makes sunscreen lotion and shares in a factory that makes umbrellas. That way, regardless of the weather, one of the factories has a good chance of being profitable. If one factory is losing money and the price of its shares falls, the loss will be offset by the rise in value of shares in the factory that is profitable.

Using optimization software, the computer runs through thousands of possible combinations of stocks and recommends, for each rate of return, the combination with the lowest overall risk (lowest correlation between investments).

When your portfolio is already optimized with three or four asset classes, you can very quickly see the effect of adding another asset class to the existing mix. If the new acquisition has a high correlation with the rest, there will be almost no reduction in overall risk. If the new asset class has low or negative correlation with the rest, the portfolio's risk will be reduced.

The most notable change in the risk-and-return profile of the average investment portfolio occurs when non-traditional investments are added to the portfolio. Some of these investments include income trusts, hedge funds, managed futures, and other alternative investments. These types of investments are structured investments and are run by an investment manager much in the same way a mutual fund is run by a professional manager. By asking your financial advisor, or by typing in the keywords into any search engine, you can find more information about these non-traditional investments. Because they have low correlation with stocks and bonds, their inclusion increases the probability of earning a higher return without taking more risk.

In a perfect world, all investment advisors would use optimization software and all clients would have portfolios that provide the maximum return for risk taken. In reality, most advisors have not invested the time and money required to offer computerized optimization to their clients.

On a risk-and-reward chart, such as the one below, risk is measured on the horizontal axis and is greater as we move to the right. We have higher returns as we move higher on the vertical axis. In this chart, portfolios A, B, C, and D are all "efficient" in that no combination of investments is available that is expected to earn a higher return for that level of risk. For investors who want a higher return and are willing to accept higher volatility (or risk), portfolio D would be best. For people who want lower returns and lower volatility, portfolio A would be best.

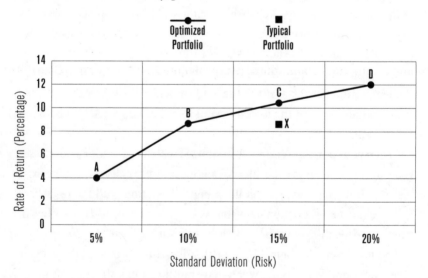

You do not want your combination of investments to give you the risk and return of portfolio X. In this range of risk and return, you could, by changing your asset mix, get a higher return without taking more risk by changing to the portfolio C mix. Or, you could get the same return with lower risk by changing to the B mix.

There are an infinite number of "efficient" combinations of investments between portfolio A and portfolio D. Here's what all of these portfolios would have in common: each would offer the highest possible return for a given level of risk. A combination of investments that is structured so it is theoretically impossible to get a higher return without taking greater risk is said to be an "efficient" combination, and this combination would be found somewhere along the line between portfolios A and D.

It is impossible to find investments that offer very high returns and very low risk. Given the constraints of the model, a well-diversified portfolio can never be above the A-to-D line. The risk and return for the portfolio of the average investor is usually somewhere near the X area. On the other hand, some of the most successful professionally managed portfolios for pension funds, endowment funds, and wealthy individuals are almost always closer to the A-to-D line. This line is called the *efficient frontier*.

The value of optimization is that it shows what changes should be made to an asset mix to bring the expected risk and return from X to A, B, C, D, or some other point along the efficient frontier line.

BOTTOM LINE: Optimization is a useful tool, but it based on historical results and assumptions about future returns. Future results may not follow the historical data, so optimization has to be used wisely; it is not a substitute for common sense and experience. Nevertheless, using optimization software as a tool is one of the best ways to design a portfolio that should give the highest possible return for a given level of risk.

WHAT YOU CAN DO NOW: Ask your financial advisor if your investment portfolio is on the efficient frontier for the asset classes you are using, and, if so, what are the expected return and risk of your asset combination.

Learn How the Experts Measure and Control Risk

Thinking that risk can't be measured or controlled could lead you to accept a portfolio that is either too risky or not risky enough to generate the return you need.

Beauty, fear, and happiness are intangibles. They are difficult to measure. Some investors think that risk also fits that description. Such thinking makes them less likely to try to control the risk in their portfolios.

However, investment risk is a precise concept that can be measured, controlled, and reduced. In this context, risk simply means the degree to which an investment rises and falls in value over a specified time period. Measuring risk allows us to predict the range of returns that a given investment can be expected to yield, whether it be over a month, a year, or a longer period.

"Standard deviation" is the most common measurement of risk. It describes the level of risk, just as litres measure liquids and kilometres measure distance. Standard deviation measures the amount by which individual annual or monthly returns deviate from the historical average rate of return of the investment.

Standard deviation provides a more precise way to measure the potential risk inherent in any portfolio. If the standard deviation of an investment is large, say, 20%, it is considered to be a higher-risk investment. If the standard deviation is small, say, 5%, it is considered to be a lower-risk investment. Historically, the standard deviation of a broad measure of the stock market is about 20%, while the standard deviation of a portfolio of government bonds is about 5%.

The higher the standard deviation, the riskier the investment. Remembering that fact is the first step in controlling risk. As an investor, you should ask your advisor to tell you the standard deviation of any proposed mutual fund investment.

If you are considering managed investments, such as mutual funds or hedge funds, it will be almost as easy to find the standard deviation as to find the price of the investment. If you are considering a single stock, you would have to work out the standard deviation yourself. If the stock has a history of monthly or annual prices, the calculation could be done in a few minutes by using a function of the Excel computer program.

It is useful to understand standard deviation because sometimes you should choose the riskier investment and, at other times, the less risky. For example, imagine that you are offered a choice between two investments. One investment has averaged 6% per year for the past five years while the other, which has had higher risk, has averaged 8% over the same time. Which investment do you choose? The problem is, you know the second investment has more risk, but you don't know how much more risk. How risky is risky? Does the higher return justify the higher risk?

If you know that the standard deviation of the first investment is 14% and the standard deviation of the second is 16%, then you know there is very little difference in the risk. You should choose the second investment to get the higher return. On the other hand, if the standard deviations were 8% and 16%, then you should choose the lower-risk investment because the 2% increase in expected return does not justify a doubling of risk. You can make a more informed decision about which investment is better for you when you know both the average rate of return and the standard deviation.

The explanation of standard deviation on page 108 is only for those who want to have a greater understanding of the mathematics behind its calculation.

BOTTOM LINE: Risk is measured by standard deviation. Over the past century, the standard deviation of common stocks has been about 20% and the standard deviation of bonds has been roughly 5%. You should know that risk can be measured and controlled.

WHAT YOU CAN DO NOW: Ask your financial advisor to estimate the risk of your portfolio.

STANDARD DEVIATION

The reason we are interested in the size of 1 standard deviation is that, in a normal distribution, 68 times out of 100, the actual return in a given year can be expected to fall in the range between

average return + 1 standard deviation

and

average return −1 standard deviation

For example, if an investment has a standard deviation of 15% and an average return of 8%, this means that 68% of the time the actual return in any given year will be between 23% (8% plus 15%) and −7%. (8% minus 15%).

It turns out that 95% of the time, the actual return will fall within the range of two standard deviations above or below the average. Therefore, in this example, an investor could be 95% confident that the actual return would be within the range of +38% to −22%. That is,

$$8\% + 15\% + 15\% = +38\%$$

and

$$8\% - 15\% - 15\% = -22\%$$

Note: Standard deviation is only one measure that can be used to measure risk. One problem with this measure is that it does not distinguish between upward volatility, which investors like, and downward volatility, which investors do not like.

Tip 38

Use "Risky" Investments to Make Your Portfolio Safer

If you have only low-risk investments, your expected long-term average return will be lower and the annual volatility of your investment portfolio will be about the same as that of a well-diversified portfolio.

Most investors with a basic understanding of investments believe that higher returns are associated with higher risk. This is true when considering investments of a similar class, but not always true when looking at the entire portfolio. For example, in a portfolio of medium-term corporate bonds, the bond with the highest return is probably the one with the highest risk. Also, in a collection of large-capitalization Canadian equity mutual funds, the fund with the highest return likely has the highest risk.

However, when you combine two or three asset classes that have low correlation with each other, it is in fact possible to increase the returns of the portfolio as a whole while still reducing risk for the portfolio as a whole.

The potential return of the overall portfolio is higher because it includes investments that have a history of higher returns. Yet the risk is lower because historically one of the investments will be rising in value at the time when other investments are falling in value.

How does this work? It is quite simple. For practical purposes, *risk* is defined as the degree to which the entire portfolio falls in value in any one period. When the fall in value of one investment is almost entirely offset by the rise in another, the portfolio as a whole has lower risk.

Using different types of investments to reduce risk is called diversification. It has always been the best way. What is different today is the availability of optimization software that can measure more precisely how effective one investment is at offsetting the downward movement of the other investments in the portfolio. By doing an Internet search using the keyword "optimization," you can learn more about this type of software. For most investors it makes more sense to ask their financial advisor about optimization than to invest in the software themselves.

A common mistake that should be avoided is to over-diversify within the same asset class. For example, it is not uncommon for investors to own

10 different Canadian equity mutual funds in the mistaken belief that this number of funds gives them adequate diversification. In fact, because all of these funds buy the same Canadian stocks, they are likely to be highly correlated and therefore provide very little real diversification. In most cases, an investor who owns one government bond fund, one Canadian equity mutual fund, one "fund of hedge funds," and one income trust would have a better level of diversification than investors who hold too many funds in the same asset class.

Sir John Templeton, creator of some of the world's largest and most successful investment funds, understands how important diversification is when he says, "The only investors who shouldn't diversify are those who are right 100% of the time."

BOTTOM LINE: If risky investments have low or negative correlation with other investments in your portfolio, they should not be rejected automatically just because of their higher risk. By combining higher-risk/higher-return investments that have low correlation with each other, the drop in the value of one investment should be cancelled out by the rise of another. The risk of the portfolio does not increase, and the portfolio still gets the benefit of the higher-return investment.

WHAT YOU CAN DO NOW: Stop using past performance as the criterion for selecting new investments. Start focusing on how, and to what degree, the proposed investment will reduce the risk of your portfolio. You do this by asking how the new investment is correlated with the existing investments. Look for investments that have low correlation with the rest of your investment portfolio.

Tip 39

Never Be Fooled by a Fund's Average Return

When you decide to buy a mutual fund based primarily on the fund's average return, you may be buying a fund that has greater risk than you think.

When investors select mutual funds, they often do so based on the historical average annual return. In the best case, they look at a five-year average annual return, and in the worst case they look at one-year returns. The problem is that one-year returns or five-year average returns do not provide enough information to make an intelligent investment decision. For example,

- The average return tells nothing about the volatility of the fund. How bad was the fund in the worst year? Remember, you can drown in a lake with an average depth of one metre. It is the deep spots that cause problems but their depth is obscured by the average depth statistic.
- The drawdown is what you should be interested in. The drawdown represents the amount you could lose if you bought at the top and sold at the bottom. The drawdown will always be worse than the worst calendar year loss. For example, a fund is having a good year and is up 10% for the first six months. An investor buys in at the end of June only to see the fund start to fall in value. By the end of the year the fund shows a 15% loss for the year, but the investor who bought at the top had a loss of more than 25%. (The fund went from being up 10% to being down 15%.)
- Look at annual returns rather than an average return. Over a 10-year period, a fund is unlikely to earn the average return in any single year. The actual annual return will almost always be higher or lower than the average return.
- Does the fund still have the same manager it had when the returns were reported? If not, the average means nothing.

BOTTOM LINE: Looking at the average return does not enable the investor to estimate the amount the fund can drop in value in any one period.

WHAT YOU CAN DO NOW: Ask to see the annual returns and ask about the largest drawdown—the amount of the loss from the highest peak to the lowest trough.

Tip 40

Ask Yourself How You Would Cope with a Major Investment Loss

Losses are always more painful than expected. If you don't understand how you will react in the face of mounting losses, you may be in a portfolio that is too risky for your psyche.

Studies over the years have measured the emotional impact on people who have gained or lost in the market. Among other findings, the studies show that the intensity of the pain and grief from a loss is much greater than the intensity of the joy experienced from a gain of the same percentage.

The joy of an unexpected gain is quickly absorbed. Investors usually adjust their financial objectives to include the unexpected return as part of their base capital. Within a few months, they have spent the gain or forgotten about it.

The anxiety of an unexpected loss can go on for along time. People think about losses a lot, blaming themselves or their advisor. They ruminate over how the loss will affect their lifestyle and planned date for retirement, what spending should be curbed, and how the loss can be explained to friends or family. The pain can linger for many years (and even longer if the spouse has advised against the investment).

A large loss may bring fear, panic, and anxiety that further losses could occur. This fear will cause many people to bail out at the worst time. To survive the down times, an investor needs to have a plan in place and full confidence in the investment strategy that is being used. Gains may trigger overconfidence, but I've never seen them cause panic. It is panic that causes the uninformed investor to make costly mistakes.

The investor who feels the sudden dread of loss is usually not alone. Many others with the same holdings feel the same way. Their instinctive reaction is to sell. This additional selling forces prices lower, which causes even more investors to want to sell. The prices keep going lower until almost all those who are nervous and fearful have finally capitulated and sold their investment.

When a financial advisor asks the pro forma risk-tolerance questions during an initial interview, the average investor, whatever answers he gives, has no real idea how he would react in the face of mounting losses.

The risk-tolerance questionnaire gives the client the false sense of comfort that he is in the portfolio that is right for him. The question to ask your advisor is, "What would have been the worst percentage loss any year during all of the last century in a portfolio with the same asset mix that you are proposing?" Since it is easier to live with percentage losses than real dollar losses, you should also convert this worst-possible percentage loss into real-dollar terms.

For example, assume that your advisor tells you that in the worst year this asset mix dropped in value by 20%. Also, assume you are retired and you have capital of $500,000. A 20% drop in value would mean a $100,000 drop in the value of the portfolio. If the asset mix being proposed to you has declined by this amount historically, you should assume that it will decline by at least the same amount at some point in the future. If you are not comfortable with this level of decline, you should be invested in a more conservative asset mix.

BOTTOM LINE: Do not underestimate the feelings of panic that will strike if your portfolio falls in value and your retirement security seems in jeopardy. You must diversify so that losses will be limited. And you should have a good idea of how large the worst-case loss is likely to be.

WHAT YOU CAN DO NOW: Ask your financial advisor how your asset mix would have performed over the last 100 years. Assume that there will be another event that will cause your portfolio to perform at least as poorly, if not worse. If you are not comfortable with the potential downside, ask your advisor to rebalance your portfolio.

Tip 41
Consider Disaster Protection

You should be prepared for anything and everything. Based on the history of bull and bear markets, you should expect that the bear market that follows one of the greatest bull markets in history (from 1982 to 1999) could be at least as bad as the average bear market that occurred during the past century.

A wise investor will reduce the risk of disaster. Most advice to investors, however, is based on the assumption that the markets will continue to operate in a well-ordered and normal manner. But what if world events lead to markets not behaving normally? For example, what if markets around the world all drop drastically and the economy goes into another depression such as in the 1930s?

If there is a global market crash, we can expect that most investments will become positively correlated. This means that they will all plunge at the same time. In these gloomy circumstances, the only investments that are seen to be risk-free are cash and treasury bills. Some advisors and books suggest that you include non-financial assets such as gold coins, art, antiques, and collectibles as part of your investment portfolio.

The effect of the majority of investors wanting to sell all of their stocks would be a surplus of products for sale with almost no buyers. Everything would fall in value. Investors might interpret the situation as a call to panic stations. The calls to their advisors would overwhelm the switchboard with instructions to sell immediately.

Although this scenario is far removed from the prevailing view, nothing should be taken for granted. Some investment managers, regarded by their peers as highly intelligent, predict that the next crash will be the big one. If nothing else, their forecasts make for riveting reading.

BOTTOM LINE: Good diversification, especially if done using optimization software, will reduce risk during normal circumstances. In a major market collapse, however, even this strategy may not be enough to protect your capital. To protect yourself in these circumstances, you may need other assets, such as cash, precious metals, and gold coins.

WHAT YOU CAN DO NOW: Read a "disaster-scenario" book to get a different perspective from what you normally hear always bullish and optimistic financial advisors say.

Tip 42

Beware of Stocks That Can Double in Value

If an investment rises suddenly in value, it is a high-risk investment; the probability of a large fall is closer than it was before the sudden rise.

Investors are delighted when their stock investments rise in value by 50% or 60% over a short period of time. However, there's a caveat. Most investments that move up quickly are high risk and they can go down in value by the same amount even faster.

This stock has most likely moved because of speculation. Unfortunately, extreme moves upward are usually followed by equally sudden moves in the opposite direction. Instead of this extraordinarily high return turning on the green light for further investing, it should turn on, if not a flashing red light, at least a cautionary yellow light.

With a properly designed portfolio, you should not expect surprises. Surprises are often caused by incorrect data, or sloppy calculations. Wrong assumptions can bring either upside or downside changes. Do not count on being lucky twice in a row.

BOTTOM LINE: If you have a stock or other investment that has just enjoyed a sudden move upward, you should ask your financial advisor to explain the reason.

WHAT YOU CAN DO NOW: Take a very close look at any investment that has enjoyed an unexpected high rise in value over the last few years. Anticipate that an unexpected rapid rise will be followed by an adjustment that will bring it to a value lower than its true value.

Tip 43

Learn How Hedge Funds May Reduce Risk

Not knowing how hedge funds can be used to reduce risk may mean that you are taking more risk than necessary to earn your expected rate of return.

Hedge funds have characteristics sufficiently different from those of the three traditional asset classes—stocks, bonds, and cash—that they are considered to be a separate asset class. The marketing materials for hedge funds almost always focus on their potential to reduce risk in an average investment portfolio.

Hedge funds are hard to define. They do not fit into a single short and neat definition because under the hedge fund umbrella are many diverse types of investment structures. A general description is that a hedge fund is an investment vehicle, often in the form of a limited partnership, that may employ a variety of investment strategies including the use of leverage and short sales.

There are many different styles of hedge funds and some do not necessarily "hedge" at all. Sometimes called *alternative investments*, hedge funds have some similarities but many differences when compared with mutual funds. Most investors understand mutual funds, so looking at the differences between hedge funds and mutual funds helps our understanding of this less traditional asset class.

As distinct asset classes, both hedge funds and mutual funds can include some very bad, overpriced, and risky funds, as well as stable funds that give above-average returns with lower-than-average risk. Just as some people lose money by buying the wrong equity mutual fund, some people will lose money by buying the wrong hedge fund.

Hedge funds can be broadly classified into three different types according to the strategies they employ and the expected level of risk and return.

- The riskiest hedge funds are in the "opportunistic" category and are described as "return enhancers." That is to say, the main reason for including opportunistic hedge funds is to increase the return of the portfolio as a whole.

- The lowest-risk hedge funds are under the "relative-value" category and relative-value strategies are used to reduce risk.
- In terms of risk, the middle category of hedge funds is the event-driven category; hedge funds in this category, sometimes called "diversifiers," are used to increase the diversification of the portfolio as a whole.

There is substantial evidence to show that portfolio risk will be reduced and return will be increased if 10% to 30% of the portfolio is invested in a number of different types of hedge funds. The reason is that hedge funds usually have low or negative correlation with stocks and bonds and therefore can reduce risk for the portfolio as a whole.

Hedge funds are not new. They have been around for more than 50 years. Until recently, however, they were available only to wealthy and professional investors. The packaging and marketing of hedge funds has changed. They are available now in amounts as low as $5,000, and many versions also come with full capital guarantees.

The following chart shows a comparison of some of the features of equity mutual funds and hedge funds.

Mutual Funds	Hedge Funds
Long-only investments	Long and short investments
Generally do not use leverage	May be permitted to use leverage
Greatest risk is market risk	Greatest risk is manager risk
No performance fee	Usually a 20% performance fee
High level of transparency	Low level of transparency
High regulation by Ontario Securities Commission (OSC)	Lower regulation by Ontario Securities Commission (OSC)
May advertise past performance	Not permitted to advertise past performance
Daily liquidity	Liquidity restrictions and initial lock-up periods

Ask your advisor this question: "What is the expected risk (measured as standard deviation) of my existing investment portfolio and how would that risk change if I moved 10% of the portfolio into hedge funds?"

Two of the best books on the topic of hedge funds are *Absolute Returns:*

The Risk and Opportunities of Hedge Fund Investing by Alexander Ineichen, and *Managing Risk in Alternative Investment Strategies* by Lars Jaeger. These books are texts for the certified hedge funds specialist program.

CAUTION: In recent years, there has been a rapid increase in the number of hedge funds that are available to the general public. In some circles, hedge funds have become the new in-thing, and as their popularity and demand increase, some less scrupulous and less competent managers will start hanging out their shingles as hedge fund managers. This poses a serious risk for the uninformed investor because hedge funds are not regulated the way mutual funds are. The hedge fund manager has the freedom to invest almost any way he chooses and the average investor may have no knowledge of what a particular hedge fund is investing in at any given time. If a manager makes a mistake—and some hedge fund managers will make mistakes—the resulting loss is likely to be much greater than the loss that would result when an equity mutual fund manager makes a mistake. When buying hedge funds, make sure that your financial advisor understands the different types and levels of risk associated with each one.

BOTTOM LINE: Most experts believe that the coming decade will be a difficult one for investors. Some experts predict that as hedge funds become better understood, they will become the investment of choice for investors who want to minimize risk.

WHAT YOU CAN DO NOW: Ask your financial advisor for information about hedge funds and read the educational materials issued by the Alternative Investment Management Association (AIMA). Their website, *www.aima.org*, also contains an alternative investment bibliography.

Part 6

Planning Your Investment Strategy

"First, have a definite, clear, practical ideal—a goal,
an objective. Second, have the necessary means
to achieve your ends—wisdom, money, materials,
and methods. Third, adjust all your means to that end."

Aristotle,
ancient Greek philosopher

Tip 44

Make Sure Your Financial Plan Shows the Rate of Return You Need

Being without a financial plan is like being in a strange city without a map. When you have a plan, you get where you want to go faster and with greater pleasure.

Decisions based on emotion rather than on logic and common sense are more often wrong than right. Perhaps in matters of love you can trust your emotions. But when it comes to investing, it is better to go with logic and common sense. Making up your mind about investments is best done when you are cool, calm, and collected.

A financial plan provides the basis for rational thinking about investments. It is a touchstone that you can refer to in order to regain your confidence when doubts arise.

Investors fall on one of two sides. For every investor who buys or sells at the wrong price, another benefits by selling or buying at the right price. You are more likely to be on the right side when you make decisions based on your financial plan.

Imagine two hikers lost in the woods. They are at different points on a path that leads to a village. One hiker knows that the village is to the west. She reasons that if she keeps walking in that direction, she will eventually get there. The second hiker knows nothing about the village. When he comes to a fork in the path, he is gripped with fear, not knowing which way to go. The other hiker knows that regardless of the dangers and difficulties, if she keeps heading west she will get to safety. At each fork in the road she is able to think logically and stick to the right path.

Similarly, in investing, some people panic at forks in the road and lose capital. Others—those who have a plan and a strategy—stay cool and enjoy the financial benefits of their decisions. Investors who stick with their plan profit by the mistakes of those who panic.

BOTTOM LINE: To become financially secure, you need goals, a financial plan, and an investment strategy. The plan will show you what you have to do, and the strategy will show you how to do it.

WHAT YOU CAN DO NOW: Ask your financial advisor for a plan that shows what you have to do, and what rate of return you have to earn to achieve your financial goals.

Tip 45
Get a Monte Carlo Analysis for Your Portfolio

It is a mistake for you to assume that your portfolio will earn the projected average rate of return each and every year. Sometimes, your actual returns will be better than average and sometimes they will be worse. Should the bad years happen early in the plan, your plan may fail because you are unable to recover from the early loss. You can use a Monte Carlo analysis to estimate the probability of success or failure.

The chart at the end of this tip illustrates a flaw that exists in preparing most financial plans. Most software programs assume that the average return is the return earned every year. That's wrong. For example, a diversified investment portfolio, which averages 8% over 20 years, does not earn 8% every year. Some years it may earn 16%, and some years it may lose money.

Let's follow the portfolios of two persons who start with the same amount of capital ($750,000), with both withdrawing $60,000 each year. Over 10 years, each portfolio has an average rate of return of 8%. For the first individual (case #1), the actual return was 8% each year. The annual income earned and the annual withdrawal were equal. The remaining capital balance, therefore, does not change.

The second person's investment (case #2 in the chart on page 127)— more realistically—made money some years and lost in others. In the first two years, the portfolio had heavy losses. Withdrawals for living expenses, combined with the investment losses, reduced its value to $399,000.

With the capital base thus reduced, income is insufficient to offset annual withdrawals. A portion of the remaining capital has to be used to fund the withdrawals, and capital is further depleted. In this case, the person's goal of maintaining the original capital is unattainable.

Enter the *Monte Carlo analysis*. A Monte Carlo analysis can be used to show how probable it is that the financial plan will succeed or fail. This simulation is able to calculate hundreds of different versions of a financial plan, with each version using a different sequence of good years and bad years. The final result is a report that shows, based on the assumptions entered into the analysis, how likely it is that a particular goal will be achieved.

The program shows a multitude of sequences of good years and bad years as they might actually occur over the life of the plan. For example, in one simulation, the good returns will be assumed to occur in the early years. In another, the bad years will be in the beginning. Annual returns in the simulations will be based on historic annual returns for the portfolio. However, whether the good years or the bad years turn up first is a randomly generated sequence.

The calculation shows the most probable outcome for a particular financial plan and asset mix. It takes a few minutes on a fast computer. Based on the asset mix, the report will show how likely it is that you will achieve your goals before you run out of money. If you are in an aggressive asset mix, one that is expected to achieve high returns, the simulation may show that there is a high probability that you will suffer such serious losses in the early years that you will fail to achieve your goals. If the Monte Carlo simulation shows this result, you may want to put together an investment mix that has a lower expected average return, but provides a higher probability that your goals eventually will be achieved.

BOTTOM LINE: Your financial plan is not complete unless you have some way to test the worst-case scenario. A Monte Carlo simulation is one of the easiest ways to get this look.

WHAT YOU CAN DO NOW: Ask your financial advisor to prepare a Monte Carlo analysis that will show you the probability of reaching your goals based on the asset mix of your portfolio.

WHY YOU NEED A MONTE CARLO SIMULATION

In the two cases shown below, imagine that the owner of the portfolio wants to keep his capital ($750,000) intact to leave it to his children. The "Ending Capital" column shows that even if the amount withdrawn each year is the same, the amount left in the estate is vastly different if early returns are negative.

CASE #1

Year	Starting Capital	Return in Percentage	Return in Dollars	Withdrawal	Ending Capital
1	750,000	8%	60,000	60,000	750,000
2	750,000	8%	60,000	60,000	750,000
3	750,000	8%	60,000	60,000	750,000
4	750,000	8%	60,000	60,000	750,000
5	750,000	8%	60,000	60,000	750,000
6	750,000	8%	60,000	60,000	750,000
7	750,000	8%	60,000	60,000	750,000
8	750,000	8%	60,000	60,000	750,000
9	750,000	8%	60,000	60,000	750,000
10	750,000	8%	60,000	60,000	750,000

Average return 8%

CASE #2

Year	Starting Capital	Return in Percentage	Return in Dollars	Withdrawal	Ending Capital
1	750,000	–20%	(150,000)	60,000	540,000
2	540,000	–15%	(81,000)	60,000	399,000
3	399,000	2%	7,980	60,000	346,980
4	346,980	12%	41,638	60,000	328,618
5	328,618	10%	32,862	60,000	301,479
6	301,479	15%	45,222	60,000	286,701
7	286,701	16%	45,872	60,000	272,573
8	272,573	23%	62,692	60,000	275,265
9	275,265	17%	46,795	60,000	262,060
10	262,060	20%	52,412	60,000	254,473

Average return 8%

Tip 46
Determine How Much You Need to Save

If you do not have a plan, you may feel that the goal of financial independence is out of reach. A plan that breaks the big objective down into small monthly targets makes the task easy, satisfying, and rewarding.

You are not likely to reach a financial goal unless you know how much you need to save each month to achieve that goal. If you don't know the amount you have to save, you have no way of knowing whether you have done enough, or whether you are even on the path to success.

When you save the amount you need, you get two rewards. First, you are closer to achieving your goal. Second, you feel satisfaction and a sense of accomplishment: you feel proud of yourself. The reward for setting aside the necessary amount each month is much greater than simply achieving financial independence. You also have the sense that you are in control of your life.

Knowing how much you need to save allows you to make fundamental choices. For example, if you knew you needed to save $600 per month to retire by age 65 or $1,000 per month to retire by age 55, you might decide that an additional sacrifice would be worth it in order to leave work 10 years earlier.

For some people, saving an additional $400 per month would be considered a good trade if it meant retiring much earlier. But if they are unaware of the opportunity, they are unlikely to act. Someday, they may wish they had known that a simple change in lifestyle would have given them financial independence five or 10 years earlier. Let's hope Carolina Edwards, author of *Money Doesn't Grow on Trees*, isn't describing you when she says, "Many otherwise intelligent adults save for retirement the same way they studied for exams: Wait until the last moment and cram."

BOTTOM LINE: You need a plan that tells you how much you need to save each month to achieve your most important financial goals. If you know what you have to do—and you are doing it—you are in control and your whole life changes.

WHAT YOU CAN DO NOW: Start the process by getting a financial plan that shows how much you need to save to achieve your long-term or important financial goals.

Tip 47
Don't Underestimate How Much You Spend Each Year

Most people underestimate how much they spend now and therefore also underestimate the amount they will need in retirement.

People almost always underestimate (and are surprised to discover) the amount of money they spend on non-essentials. They also underestimate the amount required to maintain their current lifestyles.

When asked to compile a budget, people usually list the regular recurring expenses such as rent or mortgage, property taxes and insurance, car payments and car operating expenses, telephone, food, entertainment, and clothes. Invariably, however, they offer a low estimate of money spent in other areas. Often forgotten is money spent on coffee, lunches, newspapers, snacks, alcohol, tobacco, haircuts, and medical and dental expenses.

The list of overlooked or forgotten expenditures could go on: books and magazines, cable and Internet connections, replacing cell phones, appliances, computers, babysitting, pet food and veterinarian costs, movies and entertainment, Christmas and birthday gifts, new furniture and house repairs, automobile repairs, snow removal, bank charges, life insurance, loan interest, lottery tickets, corner store purchases, dry cleaning, and personal items.

Keeping track of all expenditures for three months could be the start of finding out where the money really goes. Carry a notebook everywhere and record each purchase. Another way to keep track is to purchase almost everything with a credit card (but be sure to pay in full each month).

A friend of mine, proud to be saving money by not drinking alcohol, was surprised to find that his substitute habit, consuming special coffees at Starbucks, was costing him $60 per week. That's $3,000 annually just for coffee—okay, and the ambience.

Those who think they spend less than they do may feel safe in delaying the start of their savings program. These individuals may have enjoyed many small things, but they don't have and won't have enough for the big things, such as a vacation property or early retirement.

BOTTOM LINE: Most people underestimate the amount they actually spend each year. Living under a false sense of your true requirements makes it more difficult to achieve your goals.

WHAT YOU CAN DO NOW: Spend three months keeping track of every penny that you spend so that you can come up with a budget that is based on reality. You will be amazed.

Tip 48

Get on the Same Page with Your Spouse

If you and your spouse are not on the same page, you will not be able to focus on the most important financial goals. If you are not focused on the goals, you will not attain them.

To quote Abraham Lincoln, a house divided against itself cannot stand. Similarly, spouses divided on their goals and how to reach them will not attain financial security or independence.

Setting goals can be fun. Two people come closer together when they work toward a common objective. Conversely, financial problems can be one of the major causes of marriage breakdowns. If one spouse wants to spend on major renovations and the other wants to save the money for retirement, a compromise must be reached. You would be amazed at the odd financial situations couples get themselves into. For example, the goal of one person may be to enjoy frequent vacations to exotic locations, while the goal of the other is to buy a cottage. This makes no sense either from a financial or a vacation enjoyment point of view. A compromise has to be found to save the couple's financial security—and marriage.

If you and your spouse are stuck trying to sort out your goals, you can use the following lists as a starting point to move toward a compromise. This process should help uncover your common goals. Try to agree that, as a starting point, common goals should have priority over the individual goals of each person.

Begin by listing your 10 most important financial goals. Here are some examples of what they might be:

1. Nice home
2. Educate children or grandchildren
3. Retire at age 55
4. Annual vacations
5. Buy a sailboat or cottage
6. Leave an estate
7. Pay off mortgage

8. Accumulate $1 million
9. Go back to university and start another career
10. Get out of debt
11. Have a financial reserve
12. Other

Now pick the first five, rank them in importance, and indicate the date by which each goal is to be achieved. For example,

1. Educate children   2009
2. Pay off mortgage   2012
3. Buy a sailboat   2015
4. Retire at age 55   2020
5. Annual vacations   2006–2030

Finally, assign a number from 1 to 4 to indicate the importance of the goal.

1. Absolutely essential for happiness.
2. Highly desirable but could be happy without this goal if everything else was okay.
3. Would like it and would be willing to make some sacrifice for it.
4. If I have everything else, this would be nice as well, but I can certainly live without it.

As a partnership, you need to come to an agreement on the top three goals for the family. Prioritize them in terms of importance to you and set a date as to when you want them to be achieved.

When you have agreement on your goals, you have accomplished the most difficult step. The next step is to prepare a financial plan yourselves or work with a financial advisor to prepare a comprehensive plan that will tell you exactly what you need to do to achieve these goals.

If you have the ability to save enough each month to achieve every goal, you are very fortunate. It is more likely, however, that you and your spouse will have to come to a compromise about which goals are most important, and which goals will have to be delayed.

BOTTOM LINE: You and your spouse must talk about your financial goals and arrive at a shared agreement.

WHAT YOU CAN DO NOW: Talk to your spouse to come to an agreement on your most important goals.

Keep Your Insurance Up to Date

Life insurance is one of the cornerstones of financial security. It is irresponsible to be without it.

We should be thankful when life insurance agents give us a call. Life insurance is an essential part of financial security for almost every family. These agents provide the knowledge and impetus for us to make the necessary insurance decisions that would otherwise be postponed.

Selling life insurance is a tough job because most people do not want to face the cost of acquiring policies that will protect them and their families. In our hearts, however, we all know that making provision for the future is in the best interests of our families. That's why life insurance agents like to emphasize the long-term goals. Knowing that your loved ones are provided for is the major benefit of buying life insurance. Left on our own, however, we are not likely to think about problems, such as adequate coverage for our immediate family when we die. Knowledgeable agents can step in and explain the options and the solutions.

Yet it is almost second nature to avoid or postpone a meeting with an insurance agent. We don't like the sales pressure, and we rarely have so much surplus cash that we are looking for another way to use it. It is tough enough just to put money into a savings account, and at least when we add to a savings account we can watch our money grow—and in a pinch we can tap into our savings for something that we want or need. With insurance, the money just seems to disappear.

An insurance agent can encourage us to look beyond our short-term desires and help us see the big picture. Buying a policy that fits our needs is a major step toward securing our financial future.

If you were to speak to 100 individuals who invested in a whole life insurance policy 20 years ago, almost all of them would say they are grateful that the insurance agent convinced them to buy the policy. I believe that my life insurance investments are about the best investments that I have ever made. In fact, I wish I had purchased more life insurance when I was younger.

There are three main classifications or types of insurance policies:

Term life insurance is insurance that provides a stated amount of coverage for a specified number of years (the term of the policy), and coverage ceases at the end of the term. Term insurance is the least expensive type of insurance coverage for a young person but it becomes more expensive each time it is renewed, and it becomes very expensive for a person over the age of 60. The only reason to purchase term insurance is to provide protection for one's family. It is never purchased as an investment because the policy has no value at the end of the term.

Term insurance is usually the best choice for individuals who want protection for their family in the event of their untimely death.

Whole life insurance is also known as "permanent insurance" because the insurance stays in effect until death, or as long as the premiums are paid. The premium for whole life insurance is significantly higher than term insurance in the earlier years, but the cost does not increase as you grow older, so in the long run whole life coverage may actually be cheaper. With whole life insurance your premiums are used for two purposes. One is to pay for the mortality charge (the actual cost of paying the death benefit) and the other is to invest. Over the years, a whole life policy can build up a cash balance that can be borrowed from the policy. With a whole life policy you do not have any say in how the surplus is invested.

Universal life insurance combines elements of both term and whole life. One of the differences is that with universal life, the owner of the policy has the ability to choose what type of investment she wishes to invest the surplus in. If the policy owner makes wise choices in this regard, the final value of the policy will be greater. With universal life, the five major components of the insurance policy (investment, surrender charges, insurance charges, administration charges, and premiums) are unbundled so the owner of the policy can see the costs and, to varying degrees, control them.

Generally, whole life policies are best suited for conservative individuals with a passive investment approach, while universal life policies are more suited for individuals who want flexibility and more control over their insurance contract.

Within the basic types of insurance there are countless variations. Policies may be convertible, the death benefit may be payable on a "last to die" basis, and there may be countless different "riders" added to customize the policy. To take advantage of new policy features, investors should have an insurance review at least every five to ten years.

There is an old saying, popular among those who sell investment products, that you should buy term insurance and invest the difference between the cost of term and other forms of insurance. This may have been true in some circumstances in the past, and in some specific cases it will still be true. But today's new types of insurance policies make this less likely to be true.

BOTTOM LINE: Many new and flexible types of insurance policies are available to fit every need. In many cases, these policies will also save income tax.

WHAT YOU CAN DO NOW: Call two or three different life insurance agents and ask for a policy review. Tell them you are in the process of getting competitive quotes on your business but you are accepting quotes only from agents who agree in advance that they will limit their follow-up to one call.

Understand the Advantages and Disadvantages of Segregated Funds

Although segregated mutual funds have a high management expense ratio (MER), they may in some circumstances provide an important benefit that can give the owner financial peace of mind.

Segregated funds are mutual funds that are an interesting (and quite expensive) hybrid of insurance and investment. If your advisor sells this product to you, he must be insurance licensed. If you think this product sounds interesting and your advisor has not mentioned it, ask if he is insurance licensed. If he is not, you will need to see another advisor to buy and have ongoing service for this product. Do not allow an unlicensed advisor to dissuade you from seeking more information.

Most people who buy segregated funds do so because the investments themselves are guaranteed for either 100% or 75% of the initial or a reset value (see page 139) over a 10-year period or upon death. In addition, segregated funds may provide creditor protection in the event of bankruptcy or a lawsuit. Unlike life insurance, no proof of insurability is required. Even if your doctor has told you that you have only a short time to live, you can still buy 100% death benefit guaranteed funds.

Segregated funds may be appropriate for the following three types of investors: (1) older people who may die before the initial or a reset 10-year period is over; (2) people in ill health who may die before 10 years are up; and (3) people who may be at risk from bankruptcy or a lawsuit.

Young, healthy investors are probably not good candidates for this type of investment. In their case, the extra annual cost to run the product likely outweighs the 10-year maturity guarantee advantage. Segregated mutual funds have high management expense ratios. Unless they need the insurance, young people can follow less expensive ways to get a guarantee on capital.

Like life insurance policies, segregated funds have three additional advantages:

- Because you are able to name beneficiaries other than the estate, the death benefit does not become part of the will and the estate. Probate fees and, more importantly, the extended wait for the estate to go through probate (typically many months) are avoided.

- Privacy is assured by the Insurance Act. Unlike a will where all beneficiaries are aware of who got what, segregated funds and insurance both protect from prying eyes the privacy of your wishes and your bequests to your beneficiaries. Many people use these products to provide for beneficiaries without creating acrimony within the family.

- Cash is quickly available to your named beneficiaries. Unlike life insurance, a portion of the proceeds from the segregated fund may be subject to income tax. This taxable part is called the top-up (see the next paragraph). The top-up is the difference between the market value of your investments and your original or reset amount.

Many segregated funds allow investors to reset the value of their contract. For example, if after a year of being invested in the plan the investments have grown by 20%, you can now reset your guarantee to this new level. In a 100% guarantee situation, you can see the tremendous advantage this gives the investor. Let's say you have $100,000 in the fund and the value goes to $120,000. You reset your contract at the higher amount. Then, even if the market value drops, upon maturity or death, you or your estate cannot receive less than $120,000. If the market value on death was $60,000, then the $60,000 bonus difference is called the top-up. When the guarantee is reset to a higher amount, the term to maturity (the date when you can capitalize on the guarantee while living) is also extended for another 10-year period.

Your advisor has to stay on top of this reset feature for you because it involves additional paperwork. Be aware that because advisors are not paid extra for this service, you may have to push your advisor to follow up on the reset feature. Good advisors, however, enjoy providing this service. They seek out opportunities in hot, overvalued markets because a couple of good resets can lead to increased financial security for their clients—which can lead to referrals.

BOTTOM LINE: Many people today are selling their segregated mutual funds because they want to be free of high management fees. This may be a mistake. The fees are high but there are some very real benefits that investors may not be able to obtain in any other way.

WHAT YOU CAN DO NOW: If you have segregated mutual funds in your portfolio and you are in a loss position, calculate the amount you are guaranteed to earn as the fund increases from today's value to the guaranteed amount. Compare this return to the guaranteed return for a government bond with the same term to maturity. If you are in a gain position, consider resetting to lock in the gain.

Be Prepared for the Financial Effect of a Spouse's Death

It is not enough to make sure that you and your spouse will be okay while you are both alive and earning pension incomes. Rarely do both spouses die during the same year. If a surviving spouse is not prepared for the loss of pension income, it may cause financial hardship on top of emotional hardship.

Financial plans often overlook what is likely to happen to a couple's investments when one partner dies years before the other.

Any financial plan that does not cover the possibility of one spouse dying early has a serious deficit. The typical plan assumes that both spouses will live for the same number of years, whereas, in fact, it is common for one spouse to outlive the other by 10 years or more. They may have been financially secure as a couple, when both were collecting from the Canada Pension Plan and Old Age Security, but when one passes away and pension income decreases, hardship may result.

In the financial-planning process, the first step should be to see that things will go well if both spouses live to the same old age. The second step, however, should be to put things in place for what will happen if a spouse dies almost immediately after retiring.

Another common mistake is to assume that with the death of a spouse, expenses will be cut in half. This is usually not the case. Housing costs will stay the same, and transportation costs will change only if one car is sold. Food costs will drop, but only by about 25%. In total, the drop in expenses usually does not offset the drop in pension income.

In some instances, the surviving spouse will have the benefit of collecting the face value of life insurance. This added capital could provide the survivor with more financial security than when both were alive. Both partners should be aware of their financial situation so that they can live for the day and plan for the future.

BOTTOM LINE: Your financial plan should illustrate several scenarios, including one version where one spouse is left alone because of a separation due to death or divorce.

WHAT YOU CAN DO NOW: Ask your financial advisor to run a number of different financial-planning scenarios so that you can determine whether or not you have reason to be concerned should one spouse die many years before the other. Most financial advisors have access to financial-planning software and you should take advantage of it.

Part 7

Sticking to Your Investment Strategy

"Great works are performed not by strength
but by perseverance."

Samuel Johnson,
18th-century English writer

Tip 52

Make Portfolio Changes in Keeping with the Game Plan

Not sticking to an investment strategy is one of the most common and most financially damaging mistakes that the average investor makes. Veering from the plan is like changing horses in midstream. Investment strategies are usually developed based on logical principles, but are often abandoned because of fear or greed.

There are many different investment strategies and most of them will work if they are followed consistently over a number of years and through different investment cycles.

Examples include the buy-and-hold strategy, or buying and selling based on technical analysis, fundamental analysis, and sector rotation. Still other strategies call for diversification based on geographic location or company size. One seasonal shift strategy advocates that you "buy when the snow flies and sell when it goes." Other examples of investment strategies include momentum investing, statistical arbitrage, and buying and selling based on published insider-trading statistics. On the Internet or in bookstores, it is easy to find explanations for how each of these strategies is supposed to work.

Switching between strategies, however, whether based on an emotional response to a market downturn or some other reason, almost always results in losses. Helping you understand and stick to an investment strategy is one of your financial advisor's most important roles. The only strategy you really need to understand in any detail is the one you are following.

Investors who don't have a strategy may fall into bad investing habits, perhaps buying on hot tips, or buying last year's hottest stock or mutual fund, or making decisions based on newspaper articles.

It is a dangerous sign if you are unable to explain, at least in broad terms, your investment strategy. It is even worse if your financial advisor is unable to explain it. Whatever the investment strategy, the best results will be obtained when the strategy is followed consistently. Any proposed change should fit into the overall strategy. Just because a hot new issue has become available, and the financial advisor is keen to sell it, does not mean that it fits your strategy. Make sure there is a valid reason for every change, that the change is consistent with the overall strategy, and that the change is not simply to generate commissions or to satisfy your urge to be doing something.

Rebalancing the different asset classes within the portfolio is a move that is often called for. If one asset class has grown by so much that it now comprises more than the percentage share it was initially allocated, it often makes sense to sell some of this asset and take the profits and reallocate this capital to another asset that has fallen in value.

Regardless of the strategy you are following, in a well-balanced portfolio, some investments will always be outperforming and some will always be underperforming. The worst thing you can do is to sell the underperformers when they are low and buy more of the asset class that is currently outperforming. Investors who do this usually find that they have made their change just as the tide is shifting, with what was previously underperforming now becoming the new hot performer.

BOTTOM LINE: In sport, the winning team always has a strategy or game plan. Investing is the same: successful investors have a strategy that they understand and follow. Successful investors know how the strategy works during the bad years as well as the good.

WHAT YOU CAN DO NOW: Ask your financial advisor to explain the strategy that is being used. Whatever the strategy, results will be different depending on whether you are in a rising market or a falling market. Ask your advisor to explain how your portfolio can be expected to perform in different market cycles. When you know what to expect, you are less likely to panic and abandon the strategy at the worst possible time.

Don't Make Too Many Changes in Your Portfolio

When investors trade more than necessary, they usually reduce their average rate of return. Their return is always lower by at least the amount of the additional trading costs incurred.

Inexperienced investors frequently buy and sell and make changes to their asset mix. They think this is what they are supposed to do as investors. Experienced investors, by contrast, make relatively infrequent changes to their portfolios.

In almost every case, a change will incur a transaction cost. In addition, an existing investment usually has to be sold before a new one can be purchased. It is natural to want to buy the next great investment, whether a stock, an income trust, or a new hedge fund. However, when a perfectly good investment is sold to buy a new one, the costs may outweigh the advantages. Before rushing to sell what you already have, remember that the new investment may be unproven. What you already have may be more valuable. As well, the commission charge on it already has been paid.

The urge to sell an investment is usually prompted by poor performance, but you should expect occasional poor performance, depending on the economic climate. For example, if interest rates go higher, your bonds will decrease in value. This does not necessarily mean you should sell your bonds. In such a case, there is no reason to sell your bonds after interest rates have risen—at this point, the damage already has been done. Rates may fall again and bonds will then recover their value. The reason to hold bonds in a portfolio is for the interest income and the counterbalance they provide to your other holdings. Your bonds have performed exactly as you expect them to perform in a rising-interest-rate environment.

As a general rule, most investors should not make major changes to their asset mix just because they believe that economic conditions are about to change. Your portfolio should be designed so that different parts will do well in different economic conditions.

If you start with the correct asset mix, the right time to move to a different asset mix is when you decide to change your financial objectives. Your motivation to change could be the need for higher returns, or perhaps for lower returns (and less risk) to align with a change to a more modest lifestyle.

BOTTOM LINE: When you make an investment decision, choose wisely and then plan to hold it for many years.

WHAT YOU CAN DO NOW: Review the number of changes in your account over the last few years and try to determine the reason for the changes.

Tip 54

Don't Expect Your Advisor to Be More Capable Than a Mutual Fund Manager

If you believe your advisor is more talented than the average mutual fund manager, then you are setting yourself up to try to beat the market, while in fact you are likely to underperform the market.

If you choose to hold individual stocks instead of mutual funds or exchange-traded funds (ETFs), you are, in effect, making a statement. You are saying you expect that your advisor is going to be able to beat the market consistently without taking greater risk than the market as a whole.

Most financial advisors are unable to beat the market consistently. I recall speaking to a highly knowledgeable investor who spoke admiringly about the skill of his former financial advisor. When I asked the investor why he was not still associated with this very successful advisor, he replied that, for five years, the advisor had beat the market, but then he made some very bad calls. As a result, many of his clients lost most of their capital. With only a few loyal clients of his remaining, the advisor took up another line of work.

You do not want to invest in a strategy where you usually make high returns but occasionally lose most of your money! It is hard to bounce back when most of your capital is gone.

It is not hard to beat the market for a short period of time, particularly if you use more volatile (higher risk) stocks. It takes a number of years, however, to determine whether you actually have superior skills that will enable you to beat the market during both bull and bear market cycles. Over 10 years, it will be crystal clear. Analytical software tools can also determine whether superior performance is a result of luck or skill, or because greater risk was taken. If an advisor always beats the market, using skill rather than luck, and without taking large risks, she has an excellent chance of becoming very rich, very fast. She will also gain recognition as an expert. When other professionals become aware of the advisor's skill, her job prospects will rocket skyward. If she really is this good, she is unlikely to remain a financial advisor for long. The offers to manage accounts for mutual fund companies or private institutions will be too good to refuse.

Here are some points to consider when deciding whether you should hold individual stocks as opposed to "buying the whole market" by using index mutual funds or exchange-traded funds.

- On a risk-adjusted basis, there is only one way to outperform the market as a whole. Your stock picks must do better than the market as a whole without taking on more than the average market risk.
- It is easy to establish whether or not a financial advisor is capable of consistently beating the market. He simply has to go on record with his stock recommendations. Very few advisors will do this, however, because very few want their clients to know their true performance record.
- Even with their greater resources, most mutual fund managers are unable to beat the market index after deducting their management fees.
- If a financial advisor claims to be one of the few who can consistently beat the market, without taking more than normal market risk, ask yourself why he is not making millions managing money for mutual funds or private institutions.

Many large, sophisticated financial institutions are no longer willing to pay high fees for a rate of return that is only equal to that of the market as a whole. What they do now is simply buy the entire market through an exchange-traded fund, thereby ensuring that they get the return of the market without higher-than-market risk. The average investor can easily duplicate what these institutions are doing, which is to match the performance of the market as a whole by investing through ETFs.

BOTTOM LINE: You don't want to be paying high commissions to an advisor who is not beating the market when you can, for a very low fee, use an ETF to get a return almost exactly equal to the market index. If your financial advisor is one of the rare few who can consistently beat the market without taking more than average market risk, enjoy his success while it lasts.

WHAT YOU CAN DO NOW: Read *The New Investment Frontier II* by Howard J. Atkinson with Donna Green. This book, although written to promote ETFs, is one of the most useful sources of information about the advantages of this method of investing.

Tip 55

Don't Follow the Herd

If you buy and sell just because everyone else is doing it, you are, in effect, abandoning your own investment strategy. Following the herd is almost certain to mean that you will buy and sell at the worst possible time.

Many different investment strategies make sense if followed consistently. Yet, the most commonly used strategy is one that almost never succeeds. I call it the *following-the-herd strategy*.

Following the herd may work well for a while, just after a new trend has emerged. At the beginning of a trend, the momentum of the herd can force the market to go in the direction everyone expects it to go. At certain times, market participants will move, en masse, from pessimism to optimism or from bearishness to bullishness, and pull the market along with them.

Adventurous investors jump to buy in during the first stage of the new bull market. The more timid are held back by the memory of the previous bear market. Later, near the end of the bull market, even the most cautious investors get the bug and jump in. When most everyone believes the market will go much higher, the last of the skeptics decide to buy.

At the time when almost everyone has joined the herd and everyone who wants to buy stocks has already bought them, the bull market comes to an end. By following the herd, you become fully invested just before the market begins to turn down. Suddenly, the demand for stocks subsides because investors have exhausted their buying power. Some investors realize that these unrealistic values can't continue and decide it is time to sell. For different reasons, other investors will want or need to sell their stocks. Since the demand is now lower, investors start to reduce their asking price to find buyers.

When enough investors come to the conclusion that the market is falling, the cycle reverses itself. More of the public decides to sell to protect their capital from further losses. The herd of sellers starts to form as the scarcity of buyers forces the share prices lower. Once again, following the herd ensures that you sell your shares at the bottom of the market.

In the next cycle, when just about everyone who wants to sell has sold, those who want to buy shares find that they have to bid up the price to pry them away from reluctant sellers. This makes for the beginning of the next bull market.

Adherents to the follow-the-herd strategy might think that they are acting on their own independent opinion. What they are really doing, however, is acting on what other people are saying. They arrive at their "own" conclusion that just happens to be the same as the prevailing collective opinion. Ultimately, as just described, the investor goes over the cliff with the rest of the herd.

Better to take the approach described by Michael O'Higgins in *Beating the Dow*: "I'm a contrarian. When everyone moves to one side of the boat, I don't spend a lot of time trying to figure out what they're looking at: I know to move to the other side to keep dry." Or as Robert Prechter, a market theorist, once said, "The safest time to buy stocks is when people are afraid to be in the market, as they were in 1974, 1982, and after the crash of 1987. The most dangerous time to buy stocks is when people are afraid not to be in the market."

BOTTOM LINE: Even though it is the most common one, following the herd is not a good investment strategy. In the long run, this strategy may cause you to lose a lot of your capital.

WHAT YOU CAN DO NOW: Talk to your financial advisor and reaffirm your investment strategy. Be sure that your financial advisor is not following the herd in her advice to you!

Tip 56

When You Rebalance Your Portfolio, Do It Correctly

Without a system and a plan for rebalancing their investment portfolio, investors often become emotional and do the opposite of what they should do.

A properly designed investment portfolio will contain different asset classes that will rise and fall in value during different phases of the economic cycle. When some asset classes fall in value, other asset classes usually rise. The movement is similar to pistons in a car engine where half are going up as the other half are going down.

When asset classes are not rising and falling in unison, you have diversification and a lower-risk portfolio. Proper rebalancing of a diversified portfolio provides an opportunity to increase returns. The rebalancing process

- allows you to lock in and capture profits that will otherwise disappear as the value of the investment falls in the next cycle.
- reduces the risk of overexposing the portfolio to one asset class that grows and takes up too large a portion of the portfolio.
- allows you to buy low and sell high to earn a higher return than a static buy-and-hold strategy.

An investment portfolio with stocks and bonds as the only asset classes provides a simple illustration.

Imagine you have a $100,000 portfolio with half in stocks and the other half in bonds. During a period of rapid growth in the stock market, the stocks might rise by 60%. At the same time, the value of the bonds might actually drop by 20%. At the end of the period, the portfolio would then have a value of $120,000: $80,000 in stocks and $40,000 in bonds. Because the stocks are up in value, the ratio is changed from the initial 50/50 ratio to a 67/33 ratio. If the portfolio is rebalanced to bring each asset class back to the original 50/50 ratio, it will then have $60,000 in stocks and $60,000 in bonds.

Imagine that in the next economic cycle, the stock market drops by 20% and the bond market rises by 20%. After rebalancing, the portfolio stays at $120,000 in value because the loss on the stocks is offset by the gain on the bonds.

If the portfolio had not been rebalanced, however, the stocks would have been $80,000 before the drop and $64,000 after, for a loss of $16,000. The bonds would have been $48,000 and would have gained $8,000. In this example, rebalancing has locked in gains and therefore increased the returns by $8,000.

If at the time when stocks were at their peak an emotional investor makes the common mistake of moving more money into the better-performing asset class, the allocation may be changed from 50/50 to a new ratio of 75/25. This would result in $90,000 in stocks and $30,000 in bonds before the next cycle. This type of investment reallocation usually takes place just before the trend reverses. In this example the 20% drop would cost the investor a loss of $18,000.

The best strategy is almost always to sell some of the asset class that has gone up and use the proceeds to purchase more of the asset class that has gone down. This is the way to lock in profits before the trend reverses itself, as it always does.

To do this correctly, the investor needs to know the predetermined allocation range for each asset class. The range is set before the investor starts to worry about gains or losses. It is the asset mix that is most likely to achieve the target rate of return. When an asset class increases or decreases in value so that it moves outside of the preset range, an adjustment is made to bring the asset class back to the prescribed range. For example,

Cash	Target 5%	Range 1% to 10%
Bonds	Target 30%	Range 20% to 40%
Income Trusts	Target 10%	Range 5% to 15%
Stocks	Target 40%	Range 20% to 50%
Hedge Funds	Target 15%	Range 5% to 20%

In this example, assume that it has been predetermined that if the total of the amounts outside the prescribed range add up to 10%, an adjustment is made to bring everything back to the target percentage. Assume that, after one year, hedge funds are 23% (3% outside the range), bonds are 14% (6% outside of the range), and income trusts are 20% (5% outside the range). The portfolio components are 14% outside the range, and this triggers an adjustment of the whole portfolio back to the original percentages.

When you decide on the rebalancing strategy during a period of calm, it is easier to stick to it during periods of stress. The worst thing you can do is to let today's news and the opinions of the TV experts fill you with fear or greed, thereby causing you to abandon the strategy that you developed based on common sense and logic.

An investment strategy provides an investor with insights as to when and why the portfolio should be changed. Here are some examples of reasonable triggers that may cause you to make adjustments:

- You buy and sell based on different asset classes growing or shrinking beyond a predetermined amount.
- You decide as part of your investment strategy that you will reduce your stock positions when the market index reaches a certain level. If and when it is at that level, you reduce your stock holdings by 5%, 10%, 20%, or whatever the agreed-upon amount was.
- Your strategy calls for you to buy stocks when their price-earning ratio is below 10 and to sell them when the ratio is above 20.

BOTTOM LINE: Develop, and stick to, a rebalancing strategy.

WHAT YOU CAN DO NOW: Discuss your rebalancing strategy with your financial advisor. Be concerned if suggested changes are not consistent with the written explanation of the strategy.

Tip 57

Don't Put Too Many Eggs in the Domestic Market

Based on past experience, it is reasonable to expect that a higher-than-necessary exposure to Canadian markets will mean a lower-than-necessary standard of living in retirement.

Canada is a great country in which to live, but for most people, it is not the best country in which to invest. For the past 50 years, the major Canadian stock markets have underperformed in comparison with US and international stock markets.

Also, the total Canadian market is about 3% of the total world market. In other words, an investment in a portfolio of Canadian stocks excludes 97% of the major companies in the world markets. The odds of attaining the best possible returns, while excluding 97% of the market, are slim.

There are, however, certain sectors of the market, such as mining, lumber, and resources, where Canadian companies do represent more than 3% of the total world market. If you want to invest in these sectors of the economy, a case can be made for a higher exposure to the Canadian market.

Restrictions on the foreign content of RRSPs once made it almost impossible for you to have more than 20% of your RRSP invested outside Canada. Even before these restrictions were removed, it was still possible to invest more outside of Canada without running afoul of the guidelines. Mutual fund companies, hedge fund companies, and ETFs have created investment opportunities that give investors the same result as if they were investing in foreign markets. Your financial advisor can advise you on how to increase your foreign exposure to take advantage of opportunities outside Canada.

Let's say foreign markets outperform Canadian markets by an average of only 1% per annum, and an investor—over the next 35 years—puts the same dollar amount into his RRSP each month. This 1% higher return may result in the investor having as much as 25% more capital than if the portfolio were in Canadian stocks. For a young person starting to invest today, or for somebody looking forward to 25 years of retirement, this reality is too important to overlook.

Unless there is some change that causes the Canadian stock market to begin to consistently outperform the US and international markets, the best strategy to improve returns will be to continue maximizing foreign content in both RRSP and non-RRSP accounts. This doesn't involve moving your capital offshore to some tax haven. Rather, it means that you can take advantage of Canadian dollar investments that are linked to foreign stock markets.

Be careful, though. Many factors come into play. For instance, if you own US securities, you could create or increase your liability to pay US estate tax. For this reason, you should consult your income tax advisor before making a switch to US securities.

BOTTOM LINE: Do not limit your investments to the Canadian stock markets. You can still be a good Canadian citizen while investing offshore, because if nothing else you will be paying more income tax in Canada as you collect and spend your higher earnings.

WHAT YOU CAN DO NOW: Look at your investment portfolio to see if more than 30% to 40% of your equity exposure is in the Canadian market. If this is the case, ask your financial advisor to explain why this geographic allocation is being recommended.

Tip 58

Don't Think the Buy-and-Hold Strategy Is Always Right

An uncritical acceptance of the mutual fund industry's buy-and-hold dictum will hurt investors who hang on through most of the next bear market until they just can't take it any more and finally give up to sell near the bottom.

Jim Grant, who is a well-known stock-market bear (someone who feels the market is in a long-term downward trend) and editor of *Interest Rate Observer*, has said, "*Buy and hold* have replaced *I love you* as the three most popular words in the English language." The buy-and-hold philosophy is relatively new as an investment strategy. It is, however, one of the most widely recommended strategies by mutual fund managers and financial advisors. For the very long-term investor, this philosophy may make some sense, but without doubt the mutual fund companies are aware that they earn more fees, and administrative costs are lower, when investors stay invested.

To some extent, orderly markets depend on investors believing in the buy-and-hold philosophy. The market would become much more volatile if investors were quick to buy and sell. And there is no doubt that the strategy works well in a bull market where the general trend is up.

During a bull market, the most important factor is time in the market not market timing. In a bear market the opposite is true. The trend is down, and it may continue for many years. In such a market, this strategy may cause you to lose far more than necessary. You want to spend as little time as possible in the market during a real bear market.

To picture what the buy-and-hold strategy does for you in a bear market, consider the unfortunate investor in Japan who retired in 1988 at age 60 when the Nikkei was at 40,000. In 2007, this person is almost 80, the Nikkei is at 15,000, and the investor has lost about 63% of his capital.

In North America, if you bought and held in the late 1920s and did not sell as the market reached unsustainable heights in 1929, you would have waited 25 years to recover what you had before the crash. In the 15-year bear market that ended in 1982, buy-and-hold investors lost approximately 50% of their capital before the markets began to go up again. The loss was closer to 80% when the loss of purchasing power due to inflation was factored in.

The buy-and-hold strategy became popular again after the start of the bull market in 1982. From the market bottom in 1982 to a peak in 1999, this strategy worked the best.

Some experts believe that a new long-term bull market is under way. If so, the buy-and-hold strategy will continue to work (although probably not as well as a systematic rebalancing strategy). Other experts believe that the 1999 peak marked the end of the bull market and that we are now into a long-term bear market. Again, if that is so, the buy-and-hold strategy could cause millions of investors to lose much of their capital before the next bull market begins.

There's a quote that says, "In a bear market, he who panics first panics best." In other words, when you are in a bear market, unless your portfolio is designed to protect, you don't want to be the last one to bail out.

Some respected observers believe that the stock markets will have to fall much lower before the excesses that are still in the system have been completely purged. Only then will the new long-term bull market begin. Excellent books are available on risk, stock market valuations, stock market manias, and the history of stock market crashes. (See "For Further Reading" at the end of this book.)

If the pessimists are right, markets will go down, or sideways, for a number of years. In this gloomy scenario, many buy-and-hold investors will feel considerable financial pain. At some point, most small investors just will not be able to take it any longer and will make the call to their financial advisor with the order to sell everything. When the last small investor has thrown in the towel, the new bull market can begin. Ironically, the buy-and-hold strategy will once again make sense!

BOTTOM LINE: The buy-and-hold strategy worked well in the bull market from 1982 to 1999. It will not work if we are now in the early stages of a long-term bear market.

WHAT YOU CAN DO NOW: Read *Bull's Eye Investing* by John Mauldin for a wake-up call about bear markets and the effectiveness of the buy-and-hold strategy during long-term bear markets.

Part 8

Paying Less to the Taxman

"Next to being shot at and missed, nothing is quite as satisfying as an income tax refund."

F.J. Raymond,
American humorist and lecturer

Realize That Income Tax Is Your Biggest Expense

Sometimes we do not pay enough attention to saving on income tax because we think further reductions are impossible. But many investors overlook simple income tax planning strategies that can significantly reduce the amount of tax they have to pay.

In addition to recognizing a problem, you should also understand its impact. This applies especially to income tax. If you are paying more than is absolutely required, you may be extending your working life by several years.

Given reasonable assumptions regarding earnings and inflation, most Canadian families will pay between $2 million and $3 million of income tax in their lifetime. This is probably more than the amount they will pay for food and accommodation put together. Those with high-paying jobs will pay more than $5 million in income tax. Considering that most Canadians will retire with less than $1 million in retirement savings, these are huge amounts. Most people who save even 10% of the tax that they might otherwise pay will be able to retire a few years earlier.

By using sensible income tax planning strategies, most people with investment income can increase their after-tax return by 10%. A good start to minimizing tax is outlined in the following tips. As well, there are other ways to reduce tax.

You should read some of the excellent books on income tax planning. I think one of the best is Tim Cestnick's *The Tax Freedom Zone*. It is easy to read and covers all the important bases. Another excellent book is Kurt Rosentreter's *50 Tax-Smart Investing Strategies*.

Most investors don't pay attention to tax-planning opportunities, or note which investments are most income tax efficient. They don't read articles on income tax or ask questions. Simply by focusing on income tax, by making it a priority, and by asking questions, you will become aware of tax-saving opportunities. If you take the defeatist attitude that there is not much you can do about income tax, you may, over a lifetime, pay thousands, or even hundreds of thousands, of additional dollars in tax.

CAVEAT: Don't buy an investment solely to save on income tax. All investments should make sense and be able to stand on their own merits. However, within the universe of investments that do stand on their own, choose the ones that save the most on income tax. It is the after-tax return that counts, not the gross return.

BOTTOM LINE: Canadians pay a staggering amount of income tax. By reducing the amount that you pay, you may be able to retire years sooner. Ask your accountant to provide an independent assessment of how efficient your investment portfolio is on an income tax basis.

WHAT YOU CAN DO NOW: Read Tim Cestnick's book, *The Tax Freedom Zone*.

Tip 60

Get to Know the Tax Efficiency of Your Investments

Some equity-type investments are more income tax efficient than others. The more income tax efficient your investments are, the earlier you will be able to retire.

When comparing two different investment alternatives, investors often make two mistakes. First, they compare gross returns rather than risk-adjusted returns. Second, they compare gross returns rather than net after-tax returns. The important rate of return, on non–tax-sheltered earnings, is not the gross return but rather the after-tax return. This is the net amount that you get to keep after income tax is paid on your investment income.

Sir John Templeton, the legendary developer of mutual funds, summed things up well when he said, "For all long-term investors, there is only one objective—maximum total real return after taxes." An income tax efficient investment is one that allows you to keep more of each dollar earned because the Canada Revenue Agency gets to keep less. Such an investment can be more income tax efficient in one of two ways. The first is by the nature of the income earned, and the second is by the length of time that passes before the income is recognized for income tax purposes.

Income earned in the form of capital gains or dividends from taxable Canadian corporations will attract less income tax than if the same amount of income is received as interest income. If you are at the top marginal tax rate and you earn $1,000 of interest income, you will pay $464 in income tax (in Ontario). If the same income was received as a capital gain, the amount of income tax would be $232 (in Ontario). If the income is received as a taxable dividend, the tax will be $313. Proposed legislation may reduce the taxes on dividends even further.

As for the second determinant, whether the income is taxed in the year it is earned or is deferred for a number of years, consider this example. In a buy-and-hold strategy, tax on accrued gains is not payable until the gains are realized at some point in the future. If you are using mutual funds as an investment vehicle and the funds follow a buy-and-hold strategy, those funds will usually be more income tax efficient than mutual funds with a high turnover rate.

A high turnover strategy is one where the security is, on average, held only for a short time before being sold and replaced with a different security. When a mutual fund has a high turnover rate on its securities, any gains that have accrued will be recognized sooner rather than later. A fund with a low turnover rate, on the other hand, will delay the realization of that gain for many years.

If the mutual fund triggers the capital gain during the year, you will receive a T3 tax slip that must be included in income. For example, if you had a $100,000 investment in a mutual fund and the fund realized $10,000 of capital gains during the year, you will receive a T3 slip showing a capital gain of $10,000. In this scenario, you will have to pay about $2,300 in tax. Of course, taking this amount out of your investments will slow their growth. In a more income tax efficient fund that does not trigger this T3 slip, the $2,300 will grow in your investment account rather than the government's. Over time, just the growth on the money that would otherwise go to government may be enough to allow you to retire earlier.

Some mutual funds, and many hedge funds, do not pay dividends regularly. The entire gain is deferred until you sell the investment, which may be many years in the future.

The net after-tax return earned on an investment is not the same for all taxpayers. For this reason, most mutual funds report their gross return rather than the net after-tax return. If you are only going to be paying tax on your income at, say, 20%, the tax efficiency is of much less importance than if you were going to pay almost 50% of the earnings in income tax.

Another income tax efficient way to invest in equities is to acquire exchange-traded funds. With ETFs, you have wide diversification and also a significant income tax deferral because this type of investment has a very low turnover.

BOTTOM LINE: If you pay attention to the income tax efficiency of your investments, you will be able to retire sooner or spend more in retirement if you are already retired.

WHAT YOU CAN DO NOW: Ask your financial advisor to review the income tax efficiency of your entire strategy—especially the tax efficiency of your mutual funds.

Tip 61

Don't Turn Tax-Free Income into Taxable Income

Many investors do not take full advantage of the opportunity to defer the tax on interest by sheltering interest-bearing investments inside an RRSP. Meanwhile, many lose the benefit of earning capital gains by holding growth investments inside their RRSP.

Wisely diversified portfolios include investments that earn interest as well as those that earn capital gains. As a general rule, investors should hold their interest-bearing investments in the RRSP and their capital gains producers outside the RRSP.

One of the benefits of the RRSP is to defer the income tax on earnings. All income earned in an RRSP, whether in the form of interest, dividends, or capital gains, is accumulated on a tax-free basis. By deferring the tax, you have all of your capital working for you and your retirement fund grows faster. Income from investments held in an RRSP account will be taxable eventually, but only when cash is withdrawn during retirement, when you may be taxed at a lower income tax rate.

In an RRSP, it makes no difference whether the income is in the form of interest or dividends, or capital gains, because every dollar withdrawn is taxable at the individual's marginal tax rate in the year of withdrawal. The "marginal" tax rate is the rate of tax that you pay on the next $100 of taxable income. In Ontario, if you have enough income to use up all of the low rates of income tax, the top rate you pay on your next $100 is 46% or $46.

The result is that in an RRSP, capital gains that would have been taxed at a lower rate if earned outside the RRSP, are effectively converted into income that will be taxed at the high rate when eventually withdrawn. You are losing a big advantage of earning capital gains. It is true that within the RRSP the gains are deferred until the capital is withdrawn. However, with a capital-gains-producing investment, you are already deferring the capital gains until you sell the investment, so there is no need to use the RRSP for this purpose.

Holding interest-earning investments in the RRSP is a major benefit. If the interest is earned in an "open" or non-registered account, it is taxed annually as it is earned. In an RRSP, no tax is paid until the income is withdrawn. By delaying the payment of the tax, you have more capital working for you. Over 20 years, growth on this additional capital can be substantial.

The ideal way to allocate investments between your RRSP account and your open account is to hold all of your interest-bearing investments in your RRSP account where the income is sheltered from tax. Hold all growth investments outside the RRSP where you will get the benefit of the lower rate of tax that applies to capital gains.

Most investors have some balance between interest-producing and capital-gains-producing investments. Yet, some still have growth investments in the RRSP while holding interest-bearing investments in open accounts. In these cases, a sensible move would be a swap of investments between the RRSP and the outside account. For example, if you had $50,000 of growth investments in your RRSP and $30,000 of interest-bearing investments in another non-RRSP account, you could swap at least $30,000 of the growth investments for $30,000 of the bonds. There would be no immediate income tax implications because your RRSP is effectively buying interest-bearing bonds and paying for them with an equal value of capital-gains-producing investments.

BOTTOM LINE: If you only have an RRSP or RRIF account, you should be invested in a diversified manner. That would include holding both income and growth investments in your registered account. However, if you have both RRSP and non-RRSP accounts, you should, to the extent possible, allocate the interest-bearing investments to your RRSP account and the growth investments to the non-RRSP account.

WHAT YOU CAN DO NOW: Check to see if you are holding interest-bearing investments outside your RRSP and growth investments inside your RRSP. If so, talk to your advisor about exchanging your RRSP growth investments for your non-RRSP interest-bearing investments. There are no immediate income tax consequences to this swap because you are replacing interest-bearing investments with an equal value of growth investments.

Tip 62

Take Advantage of Income-Splitting Opportunities

The total tax bill is always higher for the family unit when one spouse pays at a higher tax rate than the other spouse. Being aware of this problem and the opportunities to correct it can result in a lower tax bill.

The objective in income splitting is to avoid the situation where one spouse is needlessly paying income tax at a higher rate than the other. The overall tax rate for the family unit will be as low as possible when both spouses are paying at the same rate.

For example, assume that one spouse is paying tax at the top marginal income tax rate of 46% (Ontario), while the other pays a marginal rate of 30%. When the higher-income spouse earns $100, the tax owing will be $46. If the lower-income spouse earns the same $100, the tax will be $30. If the taxable income can be moved from the higher-income taxpayer to the lower one, the tax saving will be $16, or about one-third of the tax otherwise payable.

There are different ways to split income. A simple approach for those in retirement is to split the Canada Pension Plan income. With this option, the CPP entitlement of the two spouses is combined and each receives one half of the total.

Other ways to split income include paying salaries, when the taxpayer is self-employed, or through loan or gifting arrangements. Also, income splitting can be achieved by having the higher-income spouse use investment assets to buy art or real estate—such as a full or half interest in a home or cottage—from the lower-income spouse.

For example, one man I know used his cash to buy from his wife a one-half interest in the jointly owned family home. The market value was $600,000. The husband, who already had a high pension income, was able by this purchase to put $300,000 of capital into his wife's hands. This transaction involved no capital gain because the family home is exempt from tax. His wife, who was in a 30% income tax bracket, paid the tax on the annual earnings on this amount of capital. The husband would have paid tax at the 46% tax rate.

The husband also paid all of the family expenses, including his wife's income tax. Over a number of years, he was able to use up his non-RRSP capital while his wife reinvested all of her income, including her Old Age Security, Canada Pension Plan, and her investment income. Eventually, they both were paying income tax at the 30% marginal income tax rate.

Some investors might think that a simpler solution would be for the husband to give the non-RRSP capital to the wife. However, under the Income Tax Act's attribution rules, if capital is given to a spouse, the tax on income from the capital is attributed to the spouse who gave the money away.

BOTTOM LINE: Over a lifetime, splitting income can save thousands or even hundreds of thousands in income tax. Income splitting is a simple way to enjoy a lifetime of income tax reductions.

WHAT YOU CAN DO NOW: If marginal income tax rates are not equal for both spouses, the higher-income spouse should start to pay all expenses, including the income tax bill of the lower-income spouse, so that the lower-income spouse can start to accumulate money in his or her own name. Speak to your income tax advisor.

Tip 63

Watch for Opportunities to Earn Tax-Exempt Income

Income tax is one of the biggest expenses you will incur during your lifetime, and the amount of tax you pay can be reduced by using the right type of life insurance policy. Although most people think of insurance only in terms of the tax-free death benefit, it can also be a tax-efficient way to save for retirement.

Deferring the tax on investment income is beneficial, but earning investment income that is exempt from tax is even better.

The common investment vehicles that allow you to earn income that under most circumstances is exempt from income tax are whole life insurance and universal life insurance policies. (Note that while the withdrawal of cash from a whole life policy is usually free of tax, a small level of tax may be triggered if the amount withdrawn exceeds the adjusted cost base of the policy.)

In addition to accumulating income that can be withdrawn during your lifetime with little or no income tax cost, insurance policies also provide a tax-free death benefit to the beneficiaries of the policy. Life insurance can help you reduce tax on income earned while you are living and can also, by reducing the tax bite, increase the size of your estate.

Investors often hesitate to consider the possibilities offered by insurance policies. They shy away from what they expect will be the inevitable sales pressure from insurance salespeople. For that reason, potential investors will often skip getting valuable information about the benefits of insurance coverage. This is a mistake and you should think of your insurance advisor as a key member of your team.

Another advantage of whole or universal life insurance policies is that you are forced to save money. In the long term, the forced savings may be even more important than the life insurance feature.

BOTTOM LINE: Life insurance should be a central part of everyone's strategy for financial security. Life insurance is an effective and proven way to minimize income tax.

WHAT YOU CAN DO NOW: Call your life insurance agent and ask for a policy review.

When You Can, Make Interest Tax Deductible

Investors who have both a personal mortgage and a portfolio of investments outside their RRSP may be missing an excellent opportunity to save income tax by making their mortgage payments income tax deductible.

When you borrow to invest in a business, or buy investments that are expected to earn income, the interest you pay on that debt is normally deductible for income tax purposes.

This means that $1,000 of interest expense will result in an income tax reduction of $460 (at the top income tax rate in Ontario). When interest is income tax deductible, the real cost, which is the after-tax cost, is therefore only about one-half of the actual interest paid.

Investors who have personal loans, on which the interest is not income tax deductible, as well as investments outside their RRSP, may have an opportunity to create more income tax deductible expense. If you are in this situation, it may be possible to reorganize loans and investments so that the interest you pay becomes deductible.

For example, assume a non-RRSP investment portfolio of $100,000 has been built up. These investments may have come from regular savings, an inheritance, or an employer share purchase plan. You also have a home that still has a $100,000 outstanding mortgage. You pay interest of $6,000 per year on your mortgage—an expense that is not income tax deductible because a home mortgage is a personal rather than a business expense.

To make your interest expense income tax deductible, you could take these steps: First, sell your investments and use the proceeds of $100,000 to pay off the mortgage. Then, after discharging the mortgage, take out a bank loan or another mortgage of $100,000. Use this amount to purchase similar, but not identical, investments to the ones that you sold when you raised the money to discharge the mortgage.

After these steps, your net worth is the same as before. You have $100,000 of investments and a similar amount of debt, either as a mortgage or an investment loan. However, the interest on this loan is now income tax deductible because the proceeds from the loan were used solely to purchase investments.

Before taking these steps, you should determine the amount of any penalty that may be triggered by the early repayment of your mortgage, and the amount of any capital gains tax from sale of investments. You should find out if the annual income tax savings justify the prepayment penalties and capital gains tax. It is always a good idea to speak to your accountant before taking any income tax planning steps.

You should also be aware that the government can change the rules at any time. A strategy such as this will work today, but it may not tomorrow.

BOTTOM LINE: If you have mortgage-interest expense that is not income tax deductible, and you also have investments outside your RRSP, there may be an easy way to make your interest fully income tax deductible.

WHAT YOU CAN DO NOW: If you have both a non-deductible mortgage and investments in a cash (non-RRSP) account, consult your chartered accountant to see if the strategy suggested above fits your situation.

Tip 65

Avoid Becoming a Prisoner to Capital Gains

Too often, investors increase the risk of their portfolio unnecessarily by delaying, for income tax reasons, a sensible rebalancing of their portfolio.

A wise investor knows that it is good to delay paying income tax for as long as possible. Deferring the payment long enough is almost as good as avoiding the tax altogether. Delaying the payment of tax until the next generation could be the ultimate deferral. This is possible through sensible estate planning. For most of us, putting off the payment even for 10 years is a big step toward achieving financial security. Today's dollar will buy less over time, so a delay in paying income tax is always worthwhile.

The desire to postpone paying income tax, however, must be balanced with the additional risk that may be involved in having too great a concentration in one security. For example, consider investors who have been advised to sell investments on which a large capital gain has built up but who nevertheless decide to hold on to the investments in order to avoid paying the income tax at that time.

I recall advising two clients to sell Nortel when it was trading at $100 per share. Both decided not to sell in order to avoid paying capital gains tax. Of course, these clients have since found that their potential capital gains problem has disappeared. They would have been better off to pay the tax and take their profit, rather than wait and see both tax liability and profit vanish.

You should avoid triggering capital gains unnecessarily. However, the tax issue should not be paramount when you wish to sell to reduce an over-concentration in a single security.

Investors become prisoners to capital gains when they allow their accrued gains to keep them from making sensible investment decisions. They know that they should diversify their portfolio to increase their safety. They put their portfolio in jeopardy by deferring, for too long, the payment of tax that eventually will have to be paid anyway.

There is also a potential disadvantage if you hold onto your securities until death, at which time your executor will be forced to sell them. The problem is that by waiting until the sale is forced, you may have to sell at a bad time from the point of view of how the market is doing. There's no way to predict whether the stock will be at a high or a low when it may have to be liquidated for estate purposes.

It is a better strategy to trigger capital gains at points when stocks are at a high value based on their historical norm, rather than to wait and have the executor be forced to sell when stocks may be below their true values.

BOTTOM LINE: On the one hand, be prudent and don't trigger capital gains unnecessarily. On the other, don't postpone too long and become a prisoner to capital gains.

WHAT YOU CAN DO NOW: Determine whether there are changes that you feel you should make from an investment point of view but that you are avoiding because you do not want to trigger taxable capital gains.

Tip 66

Be Careful not to Trigger Capital Gains Tax Unnecessarily

It is always a mistake to trigger capital gains unnecessarily because then, after paying the tax, you have less capital to compound and grow.

Investment decisions should be based on what makes the most investment sense. But when investment choices are of equal merit, the income tax implications should be part of the decision-making process.

When investment options have equal merit, and one of them allows you to delay triggering capital gains, you should choose the option that delays the triggering of the capital gain. That keeps your capital compounding to your advantage rather than the government's because you still have the cash that would otherwise be used to pay the tax.

Investment considerations should normally outweigh tax considerations. Assume that your investment strategy calls for 40% of your assets to be invested in growth investments. At times, there may be a valid investment reason to sell one company's shares and replace them with another, even though the total amount in equities is still within the 40% range, and the change triggers capital gains.

At other times, however, the advantage between the new shares and the old shares is less certain but making a change will trigger both capital gains and a brokerage commission. In this case, you now have less capital available for compounding because it has been reduced both by the tax and the commissions.

One way to avoid this dilemma is to use the highly income-tax-efficient ETFs for that portion of your portfolio that is invested in equities. When you get your equity exposure through ETFs, there is no reason to trigger capital gains unless you want to change your exposure from, say, the US market to some other global market, or from one specific sector, such as oil and gas, to another such as banking.

BOTTOM LINE: Before you sell an investment and buy another similar type, be sure you know how much capital gain you are triggering.

WHAT YOU CAN DO NOW: First, before you sell an investment with an accrued capital gain, obtain an estimate of how much tax this gain will trigger. Second, know the effect that the recommended replacement investment has on your portfolio. Is it to increase return, reduce risk, or both?

Tip 67

Use Estate-Planning Strategies to Reduce Income Tax at Death

The income tax reduction that is possible with good estate planning could amount to hundreds of thousands of dollars. Some investors seek the highest yield on GICs and always try to avoid brokerage fees but ignore opportunities for estate planning. They are like a homeowner who tries to minimize heating costs by installing weather stripping around the doors while leaving a window wide open all winter.

In Canada, although we do not have an estate tax or inheritance tax, the last year of life is when most Canadians pay the most income tax.

The tax payable at death is primarily from two sources of income. One source of taxable income is on capital gains that have accrued up to the time of death. Unless the asset with the accrued capital gain is passed on to a spouse, the asset is deemed sold at fair market value. The resulting capital gain must be reported, and the income tax liability is payable by the deceased on the final income tax return. (Note: there is no capital gains tax on the sale of the family home.)

The other source of the income tax liability is from the taxation of RRSPs and RRIFs. If they are not transferred to a spouse or a dependent child, the full amount is added to the deceased's income on the final tax return.

Estate planning allows most taxpayers to reduce the amount of income tax otherwise payable. More assets can then be transferred to their heirs or to their favourite charity. Depending on the size of the estate, the amount of income tax saved or deferred for many years (perhaps even another generation) varies from a few thousand to hundreds of thousands of dollars.

Estate planning can save substantial amounts of tax. Why, then, do many people miss out on this opportunity? Reluctance to talk about one's death, the cost of professional fees, and the difficulty of actually deciding what you want to do are the main reasons. To initiate an estate plan requires decisions and action, and it requires that you care about what happens to others when you are gone.

If you have $1 million in assets or more, you are almost certain to benefit by estate planning. Tax saving is also possible for estates of less than that amount, but naturally the saving will not be as great.

Common methods used by estate planners to save on tax include using gifting strategies, estate freezes, life insurance, and different types of trusts and holding companies. Depending on the method used, the income tax benefit might be in the form of lower rates of tax, an elimination of tax, the creation of tax-free income, or a deferral of tax for many years after death.

One approach that some investors use to deal with the tax liability due at death is to take out a life insurance policy to have funds available to pay the income tax at that time. A simple life insurance policy is one of the most effective ways to increase the size of the estate that can be passed on. However, it does not erase the income tax liability that may be due at death. Instead, it creates a source of funds to pay the tax liability. The objective of estate planning is actually to reduce the income tax that would otherwise be owing.

Estate planning is not a do-it-yourself project but requires the services of a specialist who is well versed in the complexities of income tax legislation. Contacting your life insurance agent might be the most practical first step if you want to look into estate-planning opportunities.

BOTTOM LINE: If you have accrued capital gains, or you expect to have capital gains at the time of death, on either financial securities or real estate, see an estate planner. She may be able to help you leave more of your capital to charity or family, and less to government.

WHAT YOU CAN DO NOW: Update your will to reflect your wishes regarding the final disposition of your estate. Unless you want to pay the maximum income tax, you should speak to an estate planner to determine the best way to pay as little as possible.

Tip 68

Keep Proper Records to Avoid Paying Too Much Tax

Sloppy record keeping means taxpayers frequently underestimate the adjusted cost base of their investments and therefore calculate too large a capital gain when they eventually sell the investment.

If you don't keep good records, you may regularly pay more income tax than necessary. For example, assume you invested $20,000 in a Canadian growth mutual fund. The fund realized capital gains and for three years you received a T3 slip showing that you had earned a capital gain of $2,000 in each of those years. You did not actually receive this cash because the $6,000 was reinvested in more shares. The capital gain T3 slip meant that you paid additional income tax of $460 in each of three years (capital gain of $2,000 x 50% x 46%) if you are at the top marginal tax rate.

Let's say that several years later, when the value of your investment is $30,000, you sell your stake in the fund. Relying on memory and incomplete records, you calculate your gain as $10,000 (sale price $30,000 less original cost of $20,000 = capital gain of $10,000). Based on this calculation, you will be paying capital gains tax in Ontario of $2,300 (capital gain of $10,000 x 50% x 46%).

Your true capital gain, however, is $4,000, not $10,000. If you used the higher number, you paid too much income tax. The correct calculation of the cost of your investment is $26,000, not the $20,000 you originally spent. Each time you received a dividend of $2,000 and reinvested the money in more shares of the mutual fund, your true invested cost, or your "adjusted" cost base, increased by $2,000. The amount of the capital gain on which you will have to pay income tax is only $4,000 (sale price of $30,000—cost of $26,000). You only have to pay on the $4,000 gain now because, in three previous years, you already paid tax on the realized gains of $6,000.

Pay attention to all the statements that come from the fund company; without accurate records, it will be difficult for you to recall the cost of your investment. And don't expect that your accountant is going to know its true adjusted cost base. The additional tax in this example amounts to $1,380.

Another situation where investors sometimes pay more income tax than necessary occurs when they purchase bonds for their non-RRSP account.

Typically, the government or corporate bond that you purchase will pay interest twice a year. Let's assume the bond has a face value of $20,000, and the same market value. The interest coupon is 6%, and it pays at the end of June and December. Thus, the bond earns $100 per month and pays $600 interest at the end of June and $600 in December.

If you buy this bond at the end of May, you will be required to pay the former owner $500 for the interest he is entitled to because he owned the bond during the five-month period from January 1 to the end of May. One month later, at the end of June, you will receive the interest payment of $600, so your net interest income is $100 ($600 received less $500 paid to the previous owner of the bond).

At the end of the year, you will receive a T5 tax slip showing that you earned $1,200 of interest on this bond during the year. You actually only earned a net of $700, but if you do not remember to deduct the accrued interest that you paid, you will be reporting interest income higher than it should be. You have to remember to tell your accountant of this transaction because this information does not appear on your T5 slip.

BOTTOM LINE: Your legal obligation to pay income tax creates a large enough liability. Don't pay more than necessary through sloppy record keeping.

WHAT YOU CAN DO NOW: Start keeping complete, detailed records.

Part 9

Paying Less in Management Fees

"Beware of little expenses: a small leak will sink a great ship."

Benjamin Franklin,
American statesman and writer

Tip 69

Find Out What You Are Really Paying in Fees and Commissions

You may or may not be paying too much in fees and commissions, but if you don't know how much you are paying, you have no way to make a fair judgment.

During the bull market between 1982 and 1999, many investors considered a 12% rate of return to be the minimum acceptable. They were paying high management fees on their mutual funds, but most did not object to the fees because they were satisfied with the net return they were receiving.

Today, things are different. Many industry experts predict that during the next decade, investors should not expect more than single-digit returns on equity investments. Fees, therefore, become a more important consideration. When the gross return on your investment was 12% and you paid a 3% management fee, you were in effect paying 25% of the gross return in fees. That was bad enough. But if the gross return is only 6% and you are still paying a 3% management fee, you are now paying 50% of your gross return in fees. Obviously, paying half your income in fees slows down the growth of your retirement fund.

One difficulty in determining actual fees is the number of types of fees, some of which are hidden or buried in the fine print. For most investors, it is difficult to know how much you are actually paying. This is especially true with hedge funds, which may have hidden fees, particularly if there are capital guarantees attached. In many cases, the only way to determine the amount you are paying in fees is to ask your financial advisor for a full report.

The commissions you pay on stock trades are obvious. When you buy or sell a stock, the commission charged is shown on your transaction slip. With mutual funds, segregated funds, and hedge funds, however, there may be two fees. The first is the transaction fee, which may be paid either as a front-end fee, which you would see, or as a deferred sales charge, which you would not see.

Buried in the fine print is the second cost, which is the ongoing management fee. This fee is included in the management expense ratio (MER).

It includes the management fee and other costs, such as legal and audit, advertising and printing, and costs related to guarantees and to operating the fund. The MER does not include trading costs incurred by the mutual fund. Published rates of return for mutual funds are always the net return after management fees have been deducted, and this is usually, but not always, the case with hedge funds.

You may be paying reasonable fees. If so, you should be grateful to your advisor. But you may be paying excessive fees. The solution: find out how much, both in percentage terms and in actual dollars, you are paying for your investment advice.

Don't ask your advisor for a detailed account of fees that you've paid for the last five years. The advisor will know what you are paying currently but it is too much to request an analysis of how much you paid in previous years.

Your advisor can tell you, for example, how much the "spread" or commission is on your bond purchases. The fee on a bond purchase is hidden. You purchased the bond out of the inventory of the brokerage firm. In effect, the firm buys wholesale and you buy the bond as a retail customer. A commission charge will increase the cost of the bond, and you have a right to know the cost of the charge.

Fees are necessary and investors would have very limited choices without the help of the professionals who make up the industry. It works both ways: professionals must be able to charge fees and you must be willing to pay reasonable fees. What is an overall appropriate level? It will vary depending on the size of the account and the level of service, but the normal range is between 1% and 1.5%.

BOTTOM LINE: You can't make any judgment about fees unless you know how much you are paying. Fees should be clearly spelled out, ideally in the investment policy statement.

WHAT YOU CAN DO NOW: Ask your financial advisor for a complete picture of what you are paying in management fees and commissions.

Tip 70

Don't Miss Out on F-Class Mutual Funds

If investors are in a fee-based account and they are not using F-class investments, they may be paying too much in management fees.

Most mutual fund and hedge fund companies offer their products in two versions. These are identical in every respect except for the percentage charged as the management expense ratio (MER). The lower the MER, the higher the return to you.

The MER depends on the level of costs the fund company incurs in paying the fund managers to operate the fund and in paying the investment advisor a trailer fee. In many cases, the largest component of the MER is the trailer fee paid to the brokerage firm. A trailer fee is an ongoing fee paid by the mutual fund, or hedge fund, to the financial advisor to compensate her for the service provided. The fee is usually paid either monthly or quarterly. The typical trailer fee is between 0.5% and 1% of the assets under management.

It follows that when the fund company eliminates the trailer fee paid to the financial advisor, the management fee is reduced by the same amount. The version of the fund that does not pay a trailer fee is called the F-class version. In this version, the MER is usually about 1% lower than in the regular version and the fund's return is therefore higher by that amount.

Trailer fees are an important source of revenue for most investment advisors and brokerage firms. Because of this, the mutual funds that do not pay trailer fees can be purchased only when you are invested in a fee-based account. In a fee-based account, sometimes called a wrap account, the annual fee is paid based on the size of the account; you do not pay commissions on each transaction.

Where possible, when you are in a fee-based account, the mutual funds or hedge funds you purchase should be the F-class units. If you are in a fee account and don't have this class, your advisor may be receiving two service fees for looking after one investment. Most brokerage firms will not allow this double dipping, but some do. You may have to ask to discover how much you are really paying.

When you own F-class shares, the management fee that the brokerage firm deducts each month is really not as high as it seems because (1) the MER on the mutual funds or hedge funds you own is lower than it would otherwise be and (2) it is immediately income tax deductible (if not in an RRSP account).

BOTTOM LINE: If you are in a fee-based account, be sure that you are invested in F-class funds so that you are paying one management fee rather than two.

WHAT YOU CAN DO NOW: If you are in a fee-based account, find out if your mutual funds are F-class units. If they are not, ask if the management fee is being charged on these funds. If it is, you should complain.

Tip 71

Don't Just Accept Fees; Negotiate Them

Low-maintenance investors, especially those who provide referrals, can often negotiate lower fees. Over a lifetime, a lower fee may improve your net return enough so that you will be able to retire a few years earlier, or have more money to spend when you are retired.

The price of just about everything can be negotiated. Many investment advisors will negotiate fees. It is not uncommon that some of their clients are receiving discounts while getting the same attention, advice, and service as full-fledged payers.

If you are paying for services by way of a front-end fee, or if you are in a fee-based or wrap account, the fees are generally negotiable. A wrap account is one where a bundle of services are wrapped together in an all-inclusive fee. Wrap accounts do, however, have a minimum fee, set by the brokerage firm, and you cannot negotiate lower than this minimum. The minimum fee is usually in the $2,000 to $2,500 range per year.

The best time to negotiate fees is before you have signed the papers to move your account to the new financial advisor. At this point you have the greatest leverage because the new advisor wants your account. You can likely get a better deal by telling your new advisor you will be a low-maintenance account.

Smart investors are low-maintenance investors. They don't do a lot of trades and they don't need to see their financial advisor often. The advisor will be pleased to hear that you need to meet her or him only once a year. And, if your accounts are properly set up, one meeting per year will be enough. You also could mention that you will be making few phone calls, perhaps one every six months.

It will also help if you tell your advisor that you understand the importance of referrals and that you will be glad to provide them. Some financial advisors send a small gift to show their appreciation to clients who give them a number of referrals. Tell the advisor what you would most appreciate is a reduction in the annual fee.

It is useful to know that the financial advisor can usually negotiate fees, even though any reduction would have more impact on the firm than on the advisor personally. A $1,000 reduction in fee will save you that amount but may only cost the financial advisor about $250 in after-tax dollars. The cost to the financial advisor is lower than the benefit to you because, in a full-service brokerage firm, the fees are split between the firm and the financial advisor who handles your account. An experienced advisor probably gets to keep about 45% of the total fee you pay and the brokerage firm gets to keep 55%. A financial advisor who is new in the business and is generating less income for the firm may be getting only about 30% of the fee.

Let's assume that you are dealing with an experienced advisor and your total account is $400,000. If you could negotiate a 1/4 of 1% annual fee reduction, it would save you $1,000 per year. The financial advisor receives 45% of the fee and the reduction costs him $450. Since he pays income tax on all earnings, the true after-tax cost is about $250. Most financial advisors would willingly give you a 1/4 of 1% reduction in fees if you provide some referrals.

While an advisor has some flexibility in negotiating fees that are above the minimum fee level, he or she has almost no flexibility in negotiating fees if they are sitting at the firm's minimum fee level. Below a certain level, it becomes too costly for the financial advisor to give any further discounts.

BOTTOM LINE: You can negotiate fees, and the best way to get lower fees is simply to ask for them. Financial advisors are always looking for new, good quality, referrals. Nothing will make your financial advisor more receptive to your request for lower fees than the promise of such referrals.

WHAT YOU CAN DO NOW: Find out how much you are now paying in fees and ask your financial advisor for a fee reduction based on the fact that you are going to be a low-maintenance account and/or you are going to send referrals. If you make these promises, be sure to follow through on them.

Tip 72

Don't Underestimate the Impact of a 1% Improvement in Net Return

Investors do not pay enough attention to fees and they do not know the benefit of even a 1/4 of 1% reduction in the fee rate. When you add in the benefit of compounding, even a small reduction in fee may mean you will be able to retire years earlier or spend more in retirement.

If investors knew the long-term results of even a 1/4 of 1% fee reduction, they would pay more attention to the fees being charged.

Imagine someone who starts saving $1,000 a month at age 35. They save $12,000 a year for 25 years and retire at age 60. They use this capital over the next 25 years and they die at age 85.

If you do the math, you will find that in this example the savings of 1/4 of 1% in a lifetime amounts to almost $380,000. With the same basic spending and the same income from investments, this 1/4 of 1% fee savings could mean either spending and enjoying another $380,000 or leaving that additional amount to your heirs.

This example also points out the impact of compounding over the long term and of the amazing benefit, therefore, of starting to save at an early age.

BOTTOM LINE: It is great to live in, and enjoy, the present moment. However, you should also be aware of the long-term result of lower fees. For many middle-aged investors, a 1/4 of 1% fee reduction will allow them to retire as much as one year earlier.

WHAT YOU CAN DO NOW: First find out what you are paying in fees, then try to negotiate a small fee reduction.

Understand the Benefits of Exchange-Traded Funds (ETFs)

Many investors are paying higher fees and more in income tax, as well as taking more risk than necessary. However, they are not getting any better return than if they bought an exchange-traded fund that earned the same return as the related stock market index.

"Pioneers on the investing frontier know costs matter. ETFs are key ammunition in the shootout over high fees," according to Jonathan Chevreau, *Financial Post* columnist.

The best way to explain an exchange-traded fund is to say that it is like an index mutual fund in that it represents a basket of securities designed to mirror the performance of a stock index, such as the Toronto Stock Exchange (TSX) or the Dow Jones Industrial Average (DJIA), or almost any other exchange in the world.

Here, however, are some arguments for using an ETF rather than traditional mutual fund or index fund in order to capture market growth.

- Evidence shows that the majority of equity mutual fund managers do not perform as well as their benchmark index. Over time, most Canadian equity managers will have a lower annual return than the TSX stock market index. Since the return on ETFs will be almost the same as the index, buying an ETF instead of an equity mutual fund may be one way to improve your return.
- ETFs can help you save money on the management expense ratio (MER). The average Canadian equity mutual fund has an MER of about 2.5% while an ETF has an MER of about 0.3%. This saving of more than 2% per annum is meaningful when looking at single-digit returns.
- ETFs make security changes only infrequently and are, therefore, more income tax efficient than most mutual funds. ETFs defer capital gains for a longer period than usually happens with regular equity mutual funds.
- When you buy an ETF, you are getting an almost exact mirror of the underlying index on which it is based. By comparison, when you

buy, for example, a Canadian large-cap growth fund, it is likely that you will also find cash, medium-sized stocks, and US stocks within the fund.

- An ETF can be purchased or sold during the trading day, in the same way an individual stock can be bought or sold. Index funds can only be bought or sold at fair market value at the end of the day after the markets are closed. If you see movement in the market at 10 a.m., you could buy or sell at the price at that time rather than the price at end of the day.

ETFs do not pay your advisor any trailer fee. This is one reason why the MER is so low and why most advisors choose not to recommend ETFs unless their client is in a fee-based account. If you are paying your advisor a fee, based on assets in your account, there is no reason why he should object to using ETFs instead of private equity managers or mutual fund managers.

Another reason why investors might not hear about ETFs is that many financial planners are not licensed to sell them. In these cases, an investor could get most of the same benefits by purchasing an index mutual fund, which the planner would be licensed to sell.

There's an added problem for investors who buy regular mutual funds in the hope that they can guess which managers will outperform the market over the coming year. Even if you are lucky enough to pick next year's best-performing manager, there is no evidence that she will continue to outperform. In fact, the evidence shows that after 10 years, only a small percentage of first quartile managers continue to be ranked in the first quartile of their peer groups.

There is one disadvantage of an ETF compared with an index mutual fund. When you are on an automatic savings program, you can make regular and periodic investments into an index mutual fund without incurring a transaction cost for each reinvestment. With an ETF, if you are dealing with a full-service brokerage firm, you will have to pay a fee each time you make an investment.

Another disadvantage of the ETF is that with one you have no possibility of beating the market. With an ETF, you are going to get the return of the market, no more and no less.

BOTTOM LINE: Most of the large financial institutions, such as pension funds, foundations, and endowment funds, use "passive" or index investing for a significant portion of the assets they allocate to the equity markets. These institutions seek exposure to equity markets but do so in a way that minimizes fees. An individual investor can have the same low-cost exposure to the market by buying one of many types of ETFs.

WHAT YOU CAN DO NOW: Get a better understanding of how ETFs really work by reading *The New Investment Frontier II* by Howard J. Atkinson with Donna Green.

Tip 74

Beware of the Hidden Costs of Deferred Sales Charge Mutual Funds

The real cost of buying deferred sales charge funds is often greater than is anticipated at time of purchase. In practice, what frequently happens is that the deferred sales charge (DSC) either gets triggered by an early sale, or an opportunity is lost when the investor hangs on to a bad fund in order to avoid triggering the DSC fee.

When investors buy deferred sales charge mutual funds, instead of front-end funds, their main motivation, obviously, is to save on fees. However, in my experience at least, investors who hold these funds pay more, not less, in fees.

An investor who buys a mutual fund on the deferred sales charge method pays no transaction fee at the time of purchase. And if the fund is held for up to seven years the fee can be totally avoided. There is a cost, however, if the fund is sold before the end of the DSC schedule.

At the time of purchase, this waiting period never seems to be a problem. The investor is optimistic about the fund's potential, or he wouldn't buy it, and at this point he cannot imagine any reason to sell it before the DSC fee expires. Paying no fee sounds more attractive than paying even a relatively low 1% or 2% up-front fee. In this case, the certain cost of 1% or 2% seems greater than the possibility of having to pay 5% or 6% in the unlikely event that the fund is sold before the deferred sales charge period expires. The thinking is that the DSC fee doesn't matter because it will never be applied.

This thinking frequently turns out to be wrong, however, because many investors do sell before the DSC fee expires. New and better products are always becoming available, mutual fund managers leave the fund they were managing, and sometimes fund managers go into a slump. For these reasons, investors routinely make a decision to sell the fund before the end of the DSC schedule. The fee is usually about 5%, if redeemed in the first year, 4.5% if redeemed in the second, and so on. The fee for early redemption is now based on the purchase price. In times past, it might have been based on either the purchase price or the market value at the time the fund was sold.

From the financial advisor's point of view, selling on a DSC basis is initially more attractive than charging a front-end fee. With a DSC purchase, the financial advisor makes a commission of about 5%, which obviously is more attractive than the 1% or 2% he would earn on a front-end sale. The bottom-line reason for the DSC fee is that the advisor gets paid by the fund company as soon as you buy the fund. If you don't keep the fund, the mutual fund company needs to get its money back. They do so through the DSC fee.

Investors might be interested to know that the trailer fee earned by the advisor is generally higher on the "front-end" version of a mutual fund. Typically, the trailer fee on a front-end fund is 1% per annum, while the trailer fee on a DSC fund is 0.5% per annum. The management expense ratio (MER) is generally the same for both the front-end and DSC versions. Over the long term, therefore, the advisor actually earns more by selling front-end funds.

In some cases, the mutual fund owner effectively becomes a prisoner to the DSC fee. Often, to avoid triggering the DSC fee, investors miss the opportunity to purchase improved investments. A person who had invested almost $1 million in NASDAQ-based technology funds once came to me for advice. His investments had fallen in value to about $300,000. The funds had been purchased on a deferred sales charge basis and the redemption fee was still at 5%. It would have cost him $50,000 to liquidate his investments. He felt he had no choice but to hang in for a few more years until the DSC fee expired—and to keep hoping that the markets would improve.

If your account is small and you want professional advice from a full-service brokerage firm, you should not totally reject the idea of DSC funds. A financial advisor has to earn an income. In many cases, DSC mutual funds are a sensible choice for both client and advisor. Today, however, if your account size is, say, more than $200,000, you probably should not be purchasing on a DSC basis. Five years ago, it was standard practice to use DSC funds and therefore if you still have some of these funds you should not be concerned. You should be concerned, however, if you have a large account and are still buying mutual funds on this basis.

BOTTOM LINE: Most investors with large accounts can do better than to purchase their investments on a DSC basis. It is usually cheaper in the long run to pay up front. Financial advisors commonly sell funds with a front-end fee somewhere between zero and 2%. If you are paying more than 2% for a front-end-fee mutual fund, you are paying too much.

WHAT YOU CAN DO NOW: If you are going to purchase mutual funds, rather than buying the funds on a DSC basis, offer to pay a 1% or 2% front-end fee.

Tip 75

Focus Less on Fees and More on Your Investment Strategy

Investors can lose much more by acting on bad advice than by paying too much in fees.

Fees are, for the most part, easy to understand. Every investor knows that low fees are better than high fees. When it comes to comparing the merits of two widely different investment proposals, however, a greater level of knowledge is required. While fees are important, it is the investment strategy that is paramount to an investor's success. If you have a good financial advisor, the fees you pay are a good investment.

I have known many potential clients who only wanted to discuss fees. They were emphatic that their business would go to the advisor who offered them the best fee schedule, or the greatest percentage discounts. For these investors, nothing seemed to matter except the fees. As a result, they often saved on fees but lost more by working with a less skilful financial advisor. Such investors are penny-wise but pound foolish or, to use another well-known description, they know the cost of everything but the value of nothing.

Focusing entirely on fees and/or commissions can backfire. An unethical advisor can quickly make up in volume what he loses in the percentage rate simply by recommending more trades than necessary. Even a highly discounted fee will, in the long run, result in higher costs compared with what you would pay with a financial advisor who charges a higher percentage fee but seldom makes a trade.

BOTTOM LINE: You should understand fees, but do not focus on fees to the exclusion of all other matters. The investment strategy is more important.

WHAT YOU CAN DO NOW: Find out how much you are paying in fees. Focus on fees only if they seem high in relation to the advice you are receiving.

Tip 76

Don't Buy New Issues to Save on Commissions

It is often a mistake to buy new-issue offerings. History shows than within a few months, the new issue frequently winds up trading at a discount to the initial offering price.

At first glance it appears that the buyer of a new issue avoids paying a brokerage commission. That makes new issues a popular buy. However, fee-conscious investors would often be better off by paying a commission and buying the new issue at a later date. Frequently the new issue can be purchased at a lower cost, even after taking commissions into consideration, after it has been trading on the open market for a few months.

There are different types of new issues. The most common type is shares sold to the public when a major corporation is raising capital. Another example would be shares sold to the public by owners of a business who have decided to go public by converting the business to an income trust and selling the income trust shares to the public. New closed-end funds created by mutual fund or hedge fund companies and made available to the public as a new-issue offering are another example.

New issues can be purchased only through a brokerage firm. The financial advisor and the brokerage firm get their selling commission from the company raising the money rather than from being paid directly by the investor. You might reasonably wonder where the company gets the money to pay these commissions. Usually, the bulk of the money comes out of the proceeds raised from the new issue. So, indirectly, the investor still pays the commissions. Financial advisors like selling new issues because the commissions on new issues are usually higher than those earned on a normal stock purchase.

The total cost of getting a new issue to the public is often quite high. Costs include legal fees, commissions, consulting fees, brokerage fees, guarantee fees, and banking fees. These costs are normally all paid out of the proceeds of the new issue. As a result, the net asset value of the shares often goes down in value as soon as the shares are available to trade.

For example, in the case where a company creates a new closed-end mutual fund or hedge fund, assume that 10 million shares are to be sold at a price of $10 per share. In theory, this company should be trading at $10 per share because the company now has $100 million in cash. With 10 million shares outstanding, each share should be worth $10. In reality, however, the first thing the company has to do with the money is to pay off the expenses that they incurred. After paying the costs, the company might have only $95 million in cash. With $95 million in cash and 10 million shares outstanding, the net share value will be $9.50 per share, and that is where the shares can be expected to trade.

Although this investment should trade at the net book value of $9.50, in practice it often trades at a discount to even the true net asset value of $9.50. It would not be unusual for this security to trade at a 5% discount to the true net asset value. Thus, the shares might actually trade at about $9.

If you have confidence in the company's long-term prospects and want to buy in, you could then buy the shares trading on the open market for $9.00 to $9.50. Even if you pay a commission of 2%, you would be further ahead than having bought the new issue at $10.00 without paying a fee. There is, of course, a possibility that the shares could go up, and stay up, immediately after they begin trading. It is equally likely, however, based on the history of new issues, that the shares will trade at a discount.

BOTTOM LINE: If your main objective is to save on fees, don't be in too big a rush to buy new issues. In many cases, you will be able to buy more shares of the new issue for the same amount of money by waiting until they have been trading for a few months.

WHAT YOU CAN DO NOW: Buy new issues only if you really want to own the security. Avoid this move if you're just trying to save on brokerage commissions.

Tip 77

Beware of Hidden Costs When You Buy Bonds

It is a mistake not to know the hidden costs you pay when you trade bonds. When interest rates are low, and you pay a 1% cost to switch bond positions, you have to make exceptionally good calls in order to be further ahead after the trade.

You don't see the fee that you pay when you purchase government or corporate bonds. If you want to know the cost, you should ask your advisor.

Government or corporate bonds are usually purchased out of the inventory that the brokerage firm owns. In this case, the brokerage firm is acting as a principal rather than as your agent. It is like going into a store and purchasing goods from the store's inventory. The brokerage firm makes money by buying bonds on the open market at a wholesale price and then selling to you at a retail.

By way of comparison, when you purchase stocks, the brokerage firm usually, but not always, is acting as your agent. In this case, the firm is buying the shares on your behalf in the same way that a real estate agent helps you buy a house owned by a third party.

On bonds, the cost or "spread" (the difference between the wholesale price and the retail price) is built into the retail price. You do not see how much you pay. The financial advisor involved in the trade enters into the computer the level of fee that will be charged and you are told what the yield will be based on this charge. A typical fee (also referred to as a "commission") is 0.5% to 1%, but discounts may be available if you ask.

The fee or commission is generally calculated on the face value, or maturity value, of the bond. The commissions on a long-term strip bond can therefore be huge. If you spend $10,000 for a strip bond that will mature at $35,000 in 25 years' time, and you pay a 1% commission on the maturity value of $35,000, you are effectively paying a 3.5% commission on the actual purchase price. (See the note on strip bonds on the next page.)

Occasionally, it may make sense to alter the makeup of your bond portfolio to anticipate changes in interest rates. However, if your portfolio is properly diversified, you are generally better off holding the bonds to maturity.

Your financial advisor and the brokerage firm make excellent commissions when there is a lot of trading activity in bonds. For you to make money by trading bonds, your advisor needs to make consistently accurate predictions—in advance of other professionals—as to where interest rates are heading. I would question why an advisor with this level of skill is working in the retail market and not running a fixed-income arbitrage strategy for a hedge fund.

NOTE: Strip bonds do not pay interest but are purchased at a deep discount to their face value. The return you receive from strip bonds is the appreciation in price from the time you make the purchase until the time you sell or the bond matures. Strip bonds are suitable for registered accounts but usually not for non-registered accounts. Strip bonds are not practical for non-registered accounts because the increase in value is taxed as interest even though no interest payments have been received. It is also sometimes difficult to try to work out the amount that should be included in taxable income.

BOTTOM LINE: When you trade bonds, unseen fees or commissions can have the effect of reducing the rate of return that you might otherwise earn. Over the long term, because of the hidden costs, most investors will find that using an active trading strategy does not improve the net return over a buy-and-hold strategy.

WHAT YOU CAN DO NOW: Ask your financial advisor for the details on the spread, or commission rate, on your bond purchases.

Tip 78

Don't Try to Make Capital Gains on Your Bonds

When investors try to increase their total after-tax return by actively trading bonds, they will certainly increase commissions paid, but it is less likely that they will also be able to increase the total net return.

When investors own government or corporate bonds, they see the market value of the bonds constantly changing. The changes in market value are primarily, but not entirely, in response to changing interest rates.

An increase in interest rates by the central bank brings a decrease in the market value of bonds. A bond with an existing fixed rate of interest—whatever it might be—is less attractive in a higher interest rate environment. Conversely, when interest rates decrease, the bonds that you already own will increase in value.

Investors are sometimes tempted, or encouraged by their financial advisor, to sell the bonds that have risen in value to realize the accrued profit. They may see an opportunity to increase their profits by following a strategy of buying bonds when interest rates in the economy are high and selling them when rates are lower. By buying low (when interest rates are high) and selling high (when interest rates are low), investors earn capital gains in addition to annual interest.

The strategy rarely works for three reasons: commission costs, the inability to consistently predict where interest rates will go, and the need to reinvest at prevailing rates. If you buy a bond and hold it to maturity, you will earn the rate of return you expected to earn when you first bought the bond, regardless of how interest rates have changed in the meantime. When investors understand this, it is easier for them to ignore the monthly or quarterly fluctuations in their bond portfolio because they know their bonds will almost always mature at their face value.

Given that interest rates rise and fall over economic cycles, the chances for capital losses or gains are about equal. Extensive studies have shown that over 90% of all the return earned by investing in bonds comes from interest payments. The other 10% is from capital gains. In other words, if the average return from investing in bonds was 5%, then 4.5% was earned from the interest coupons and 0.5% was earned from trading.

Some people may believe that this average improvement of the expected return is worth the costs of active trading. I believe there is almost no chance that the average investor will benefit by actively trading bonds. Consider that the professional traders expect to improve the rate of return by only about 1% per annum, and they buy wholesale rather than retail and buy and sell with lower commissions than the average investor. However, I suggest that if an investor wants to try to increase the return on bonds, he or she should use a bond mutual fund with a very low MER.

It is also questionable whether it makes sense to sell a bond at a profit, trigger the tax immediately, and then take the money and invest in bonds with a similar term to maturity but at a lower interest rate. Some see a benefit in earning a capital gain, as opposed to interest, but this benefit is partly offset by the disadvantage of paying tax sooner than necessary and by paying commissions.

There are two occasions when the sensible thing might be to sell bonds that have risen in value: when you want to move out of the bond asset class altogether, or when you want to make a significant shift in the "duration" of your bond portfolio.

Duration is a more precise way to measure the average term to maturity of your bond portfolio. Duration takes into consideration not only the number of years before the bond matures but also the interest payments that you will receive. When the coupon interest rate is high, your cash flow is higher, which means you receive that portion of your money sooner. The faster your capital is returned, the shorter the duration of the bond.

BOTTOM LINE: Professional bond traders and fixed-income arbitrage specialists find it difficult to make capital gains by trading bonds in anticipation of interest rate changes, and they pay almost nothing in commissions. Given the high commissions that you pay, you are generally better off holding your bonds to maturity.

WHAT YOU CAN DO NOW: If your financial advisor suggests that you sell a bond to take a profit—but you then have to invest the proceeds in a bond with a lower yield—ask for a calculation that compares the total after-tax return of the bond that you now have with the expected total after-tax return for the new bond that you will purchase with the proceeds.

Tip 79

Understand the Costs of Buying or Selling Thinly Traded Stocks

Some investors trade too much for their own good because they are unaware of the hidden costs of trading, particularly if they are trading in stocks that move on low volumes (thinly traded stocks).

You should be aware of three trading costs on stocks that trade on low volumes.

The commission is the first and most visible of these three costs. and it is therefore the focus for most investors. Although less visible, the other costs are often greater and can result in a penalty for frequent buyers or sellers of low-volume stocks.

The second cost is the difference between the bid price and the asking price for a stock. Assume that the last trade on a stock was $10. The new bid price—the price someone is willing to pay to buy the stock—might be $9.80. On the other side, the price asked by someone who is willing to sell or "offer" the stock is $10.20. This difference is called the *spread* and represents the potential profit for the market maker. The market maker is the person or firm taking the responsibility of buying and selling as necessary to create a ready market for the stock.

In effect, the market maker gives the offering price to the seller, and charges the asking price to the buyer. On thinly traded stocks, the spread might be 2% to 5% of the purchase price. In this instance, the buyer at $10.20 is paying 40 cents more for the shares than he could get for them if he resold them immediately. A frequent buyer or seller of thinly traded stocks loses the amount of the spread every time he or she buys or sells.

The third cost is the amount by which your trade moves the market. For example, assume that you want to purchase 10,000 shares of a thinly traded stock trading at $10, with a bid price of $9.80 and an asking price of $10.20. Placing an order to purchase 10,000 shares is likely going to cause the share price to increase. You might be able to buy 1,000 shares from the first individual who was offering to sell her shares at $10.20, but to get the rest of the shares that you want, you will have to increase the price in order to interest the other shareholders in selling. In effect, it is your buying that is causing the share price to move higher, and this is an added cost to you.

The hidden cost of the spread and the cost of the movement in the market are generally greater than the cost of the commission that the brokerage firm receives. These costs are not a factor, however, when you purchase large-capitalization companies that are traded on the New York Stock Exchange (NYSE). With large-capitalization, high-volume stocks, there is usually only a very small difference between the bid and the ask price, and your order has no impact on the movement of the price.

BOTTOM LINE: Do not focus entirely on the commission being charged each time you trade stocks. This is only one of the costs you pay and it may not be the largest. A skilful financial advisor who understands the market can do a lot to reduce the other costs of trading in low-volume shares.

WHAT YOU CAN DO NOW: The next time you make a trade, note the difference between the bid and the ask price before the transaction, and then again after the trade has been filled. You should also ask your advisor to check the bid and ask price and the volume being traded before you place your order.

Part 10

Betting on the Tortoise, not the Hare

"The remedy is for people to stop watching the ticker,
listening to the radio, drinking bootleg gin, and dancing to
jazz; forget the 'new economics' and prosperity founded upon
spending and gambling, and return to the old economics and
prosperity based upon savings and working."

Thomas W. Lamont,
New York banker and partner of J.P. Morgan & Co.

Tip 80
Practise the Virtue of Patience

Impatience causes investors to buy and sell before giving an investment a chance to perform. It takes 20 to 30 years to grow a large oak tree, and for most of us it will take the same length of time investing before we are financially independent.

Patience is an important quality needed to attain financial security and wealth. It is, however, rarely found among average investors. Its value is almost always underestimated. Patience is required to make the magic of compounding interest work. Einstein is reported to have said that the "magic" of compounding interest should be the eighth wonder of the world.

Brokerage firms sometimes profit by dealing with people who lack patience and who want to earn high returns fast. These firms, and some financial advisors, love the investors who lack patience, because their financial habits generate huge commissions. Such investors might buy excellent-quality shares and sell them a few months later for other shares because the original batch didn't rise as quickly as expected. This sale generates two commissions for the brokerage firm and is unlikely to benefit the client.

There's a parallel between our physical and financial health. Most people accept that good health and fitness don't come at the snap of a finger but require watching your diet, working out regularly, and doing everything in moderation. Impatient people turn to steroids.

The way to practise patience is to keep the objectives of your financial plan in mind. When you are confident that your plan will work out, it is easier to be patient.

We are in no hurry to get old because we all get old fast enough. In the same way, wealth will come quickly enough if we are patient and follow our financial plan and investment strategy.

It is not hard to be patient if you are following a plan that you are confident will bring success. The least complicated strategy is the best: the strategy of saving 10% of what you earn. If you get into this habit when you are young, it will lead to financial security over time.

BOTTOM LINE: Your safe and well-diversified investment portfolio should be designed to earn the rate of return you need for your financial goals. Be patient. Let the magic of compounding do its work.

WHAT YOU CAN DO NOW: Ensure that your portfolio is designed to earn slow and steady returns while avoiding significant losses. Exercise patience and let the portfolio grow according to plan. Don't think that you can accelerate the rate of return without increasing the risk.

Tip 81

Don't Check Your Portfolio Every Day

Looking at the market every day makes you want to make changes more frequently than necessary. Buying or selling based on impulse usually means buying high, selling low, incurring too much in trading costs, and generally reducing your return.

Warren Buffett says it would be fine by him if the stock market was open for trading only one day each year. Buffett, one of the most perceptive investors in the world, says it is not necessary to pay attention to the daily stock market movements, and not profitable to trade daily. This prompts the question, Why are most investors looking at the market virtually every day?

It might make sense to look at the market every day if you are trading based on short-term fluctuations. However, in the long run, most day traders lose all their money. This happens even though their trading carries a low cost per transaction. For the average investor, who incurs a larger transaction cost, day trading makes even less sense. The exception is the financial advisor who makes a commission on every trade.

The historical record of stock trading and Modern Portfolio Theory give us two really clear lessons about investing in the stock market.

Lesson number one: Investments usually rise in value when they are held for long periods of time. Having a portion of one's capital invested in these long-term investments makes good sense for most people. Even if you would like to be 100% in government bonds, you can have lower overall risk if you add some common stock equity investments to your portfolio.

Lesson number two: For investors, short-term trading costs money. Generally, the only beneficiaries of short-term trading are firms and individuals who make commissions on each of your trades.

If you look at your asset mix once a year, and make the necessary adjustments to bring the asset allocation back to the desired mix, you will have a better result than if you buy and sell on a regular basis. Frequent changes usually cost money and could reduce the overall return.

BOTTOM LINE: If you have a well-diversified portfolio, you don't need to look at it more than once each quarter.

WHAT YOU CAN DO NOW: If your portfolio is not properly diversified, make it so, and then resolve to look it at only once a quarter.

Tip 82

Understand When Market Timing Does Work

It is a mistake to think that it is impossible to judge whether the market is overvalued or undervalued by historical measurements. The market's current price–earnings ratio is available with a few clicks on the S&P 500 website.

Sir John Templeton wisely stated that "bull markets are born on pessimism, grow on skepticism, mature on optimism and die on euphoria."

Almost every professional in the industry tells clients not to try to time the market. By "timing the market," we mean delaying the planned purchase of an investment because you expect the market to fall or delaying the planned sale of an investment because you expect the market to rise.

Most experts seem to agree that what counts is time in the market, not timing the market. What's important is the number of years your capital has compounded, not the price on the day that you made your purchase. However, the answer is not as simple as some would suggest.

Success with market timing depends largely on the time frame over which you are going to measure success or failure. If you are trying to time the market over the short term—over a period of less than five years—market timing rarely works. However, if you look at a 15-year period, the case for market timing is compelling.

Nortel provides an obvious illustration that it is always better to buy when share prices are low, say $4, than when they are high at $120. If market timing doesn't work, then it would make no difference to one's ultimate return whether you bought Nortel at $120 or $4. Clearly it does make a difference. The question is, how do you know whether a share, or the market in total, is cheap or expensive? In the short term, and for short holding periods (less than five years), it is impossible to tell. However, a look at the past century of the market reveals useful statistics that indicate whether stocks are cheap or expensive by historical measures.

There are a number of excellent books on market timing and one of the best and easiest to read is *Yes, You Can Time the Market!* by Ben Stein and Phil DeMuth. The following examples have been adapted from this book. The authors show that, over the long term, your return will be better if you invest when the market is undervalued by historical standards than if you invest when it is overvalued. The measurement tools to tell you whether it is undervalued or overvalued include the price–earnings ratio, the dividend yield ratio, and the fundamental value (or Tobin's Q) ratio. Explanations for these ratios may be found in the book and on almost any financial website.

Stein and DeMuth have a table showing the price–earnings ratio of the S&P 500 Index for the past 100 years. You can see which years had the highest price–earnings ratios and compare them with those with the lowest ratios. It then is easy to compare, over a 15-year period, the results of buying shares when the price–earnings ratio was in the top 25% of all the years, with the results of buying shares in the years when the price–earnings ratio was in the bottom 25%. The comparison shows that by buying when the price–earnings ratio was low, the total average improvement in return is about 10% per annum.

When the stock market is overvalued by historical measures, the smartest thing is to be patient. Wait until the market is undervalued by historical measures. You may have to wait for a few years, but in the long term, being patient when markets are overvalued is very wise.

BOTTOM LINE: While it is impossible for most investors, or advisors, to time the market in the short term, it is possible and practical to do so if you measure success over a 15- to 20-year period.

WHAT YOU CAN DO NOW: Read Stein and DeMuth's book *Yes, You Can Time the Market!* and ask your financial advisor how the current values for the above ratios compare with the long-term average values for these ratios for the market as a whole.

Tip 83

Base Decisions on Your Plan, not Your Emotions

Not having a plan is like driving in the dark without headlights. When you have a plan and an investment strategy, you can avoid panic during a market crisis and greed during a speculative bubble.

Investors would do better if they understood how professional investment managers invest in a dispassionate and objective manner.

Professional investment managers usually welcome a volatile market because they make profits at the expense of those investors who fret and worry about the ups and downs of the market. This is a situation where the pros sell high to panicky investors who want to buy because everyone else appears to be buying. By the same reasoning, they buy low from equally distressed investors who want to sell because everyone else seems to be selling.

Those skilled in the financial industry know what to expect in terms of volatility. Usually their investment decisions are based on facts and detailed analysis rather than hunches. The *Star Trek* heroes Spock and Data would have made good investors because they would have been able to follow their investment strategy coolly and rationally. The best finance professionals are successful because they are able to operate with a cool and analytic approach. They can operate this way because

- they understand the market and know that volatility is not something to panic over but to welcome.
- they have a plan or investment strategy and they follow it. When the market goes up, they execute certain aspects of the plan; when the market goes down, they execute other aspects. In some cases, the plan is applied by a computer program.
- they are not using their money and their own financial health is not at stake. Individual investors are under much greater pressure and often are concerned about their retirement plans. This explains why some individuals let the instincts of fear and greed dictate their investment decisions. When investors let these subjective concerns influence their decisions, they usually buy or sell at the wrong time.

To avoid buying at the top and selling at the bottom of the market, you should have a financial plan that tells you what rate of return you need to earn to achieve your goals, and an investment strategy that can reasonably be expected to earn that rate of return over time.

Assume that you have a financial plan that tells you that you need to earn, on average, 8% in order to be able to retire when you want to. You are in an investment portfolio that is designed to make, on average, 8%. In this example, you know that the portfolio is expected to deliver returns in the range of –8% to +24%, with 8% being the most likely return. As a result, you are less likely to panic when the portfolio has a bad year and delivers a negative return—one within the range of returns you expect. You would always prefer a positive return, but as long as the market is performing the way you expect it to, you're okay. With that self-assurance, you will also avoid the desire to jump on a speculative bandwagon when the market is near its peak.

BOTTOM LINE: A financial plan and an investment strategy are needed to keep you on course. Without a plan and strategy, you will be tempted to react emotionally—and emotional reactions are usually wrong.

WHAT YOU CAN DO NOW: Get a financial plan that tells you the return you need, and have an investment strategy that is designed to make, on average, that return.

Tip 84

Never Be Fooled by the Recent Track Records of Stocks and Funds

Buying last year's hottest fund is usually a bad idea. After all, its growth has already occurred. It is much better for investors to be in a fund where the capital growth is in the future, not the past.

Rule 6 of Peter Wyckoff's 32 rules for investing is, "The worst losses in the market come from uninformed people buying greatly overvalued stocks."

It is easy to find statistics that show which fund gave the best return last year. What is more important, and much more difficult, is to determine which fund will have the best return next year.

In order to find next year's best-performing fund, or at least a fund that will be in the top quartile of similar funds, past performance can be an important guide. However, experienced and novice investors often react differently to past performance statistics. Those new to the market will look for the mutual fund that had the best performance last year and then put their money in that fund. Investors who have been around longer are more apt to move their money to last year's worst-performing mutual fund (if this fund has in its past demonstrated superior performance).

Several studies have compared the results of moving money on the first of January into the previous year's worst-performing mutual fund with the results of moving to the previous year's best-performing fund. The studies show that an investor would usually be better off by choosing last year's worst rather than last year's best.

Before rushing to buy last year's worst performers, however, you should understand why last year's best-performing manager may perform poorly in the following year. There are a number of reasons, and one is that this manager may be swamped with new cash to invest in the following year. As many investors move money to last year's hottest fund, the manager of that fund will find it more difficult to invest a large amount of cash with the same results that were possible with a smaller pool of capital.

When a fund is small, the manager can be quick to take advantage of opportunities without moving the market. A larger fund can't move as quickly because its buy and sell orders are larger. The buy order itself creates so much demand that the price of the shares being purchased often goes up before the purchase is complete. Putting so many shares on the market is itself a cause of the price going down and so the fund may get a lower price when it sells.

Underperformance may also result from misjudging which sector of the economy will be next year's "hot" sector. If the manager did exceptionally well one year, it might be because he had a sizeable amount of the fund invested in the economy's hot sector before that sector became hot. In the following year, to continue with his above-average performance, the manager has to move out of that sector and find the next hot sector before it starts to rise. This is difficult to do. Last year's underperforming manager made the wrong pick for what would be the hot sector. As a result, he had too much invested in a slow sector.

Last year's underperforming manager may not have to make any changes in her portfolio to be in the current year's hottest sector because she is already there. Last year's hottest manager has to move a lot of money into the "about to become hot" sector. The timing issues and the costs to make this change will make it less likely that he will be the top performer for two years in a row.

Be aware, however, that a number of bad years in a row may indicate that the underperforming manager has lost her touch. You should stay away from a fund where the yearly results and the three-year and five-year results are consistently poor.

Funds are frequently ranked according to whether they are in the first quartile, that is, better than 75% of the funds in their peer group, or the second quartile, and so on. Funds in the fourth quartile have lower performance than 75% of their peer group. The kind of underperforming fund that you should look for is one where the manager is above average over three- and five-year periods but has underperformed only in the most recent year or quarter. You should make sure the current manager is the same person who was there when the good returns were earned.

BOTTOM LINE: Don't look in the newspaper and decide to invest based on very short-term performance over the past quarter, or even the past year.

A fund that can go up by 30% in a few months can also fall by 30% in the same length of time.

WHAT YOU CAN DO NOW: If you are going to buy a mutual fund, first look to the under-performers. Call the company to get the explanation as to why the fund's recent performance is below average. If you are satisfied with the response, buy this fund rather than last year's or, worse, last quarter's hottest fund.

Tip 85

Don't Get Stuck Thinking That the Current Trend Will Continue

It is a mistake to believe the short-term trend will continue. It always reverses itself. An investor who buys assuming that the short-term trend will continue going up is usually buying high. Selling when the short-term trend is down usually means selling low.

As emphasized throughout this book, investors regularly lose money because they focus on the current short-term trend in the stock market and ignore the larger perspective and longer-term trend. The stock market almost never moves in a straight line. The short-term trend usually reverses itself just when most investors believe it is almost certain to continue. In spite of the fact that this has been proved in countless studies, investors still are most likely to invest when the majority is in agreement that the markets are going to go higher.

However, the experienced investor knows that whatever the current trend is does not make much difference. This investor is not unduly influenced by the consensus opinion and not likely to rush to make changes in the portfolio.

This leads us to consider the type of investor known as the "contrarian." The contrarian is simply one who does not accept the majority view. When almost everyone believes the market is going to continue on its present path, the contrarian takes the opposite view. The contrarian, over the long run, is almost always right.

A century of past performance shows that, at the point where the market changes from bull to bear or vice versa, the general public and experts alike are usually wrong. The market usually starts heading down at the point of maximum optimism or up at the point of maximum fear. The contrarian knows this and instead of doing what most experts recommend, does the opposite.

The public does exert a major influence on the market. When a majority of investors believe in the market and decide to invest, they can push the market up for a number of years. In a bull market, the danger point comes when almost everyone is thinking the same way. At this point, almost everyone has already jumped in, and so there are fewer investors who can buy and keep the market going higher. Just when people are most euphoric, or most in despair, is when public opinion fails. This is the time when the contrarian makes his bet against the public.

BOTTOM LINE: Don't be too concerned about the short-term trend. If the market is on fire and seems to be going straight up, wait for a while and you will have a chance to buy when it pulls back. If it seems the market is collapsing, wait for a while and you will probably have an opportunity to sell, at a better price, when the market rallies.

WHAT YOU CAN DO NOW: Read one of the following books on market psychology: *Investment Psychology Explained* by Martin J. Pring, *Bull's Eye Investing* by John Mauldin, or *Socionomics* by Robert Prechter.

Tip 86

Don't Use Short-Term Investments for Long-Term Goals and Vice Versa

Investors who use a short-term vehicle for a long-term goal may not earn enough to reach the goal. Conversely, long-term investments, such as common stocks, should never be used for short-term goals, because these investments might fall by 20% to 40% before you need the money.

Long-term goals are best achieved through long-term investments. Similarly, short-term investments are best when accumulating or saving capital for a near-term need. As simple as this sounds, uninformed investors often acquire the wrong investment for a specific goal they have in mind. The following guideline could be useful for investors new to the market.

Equity investments—investments in the common stock of publicly traded companies—are long-term investments and should be used to save for the future and for retirement. Similarly, whole and universal life insurance are long-term investments. Investments such as treasury bills and savings accounts are short-term investments and should be used for more immediate needs, such as saving for the down payment for a house.

Over long periods of time, equities usually produce a return higher than investing in treasury bills, guaranteed investment certificates, or bonds. With this higher return comes higher volatility. For that reason, equities should not be used for short-term goals.

Equities can fall in value by 20% to 40% or more during a severe stock market downturn. If you might need money quickly, it could be disastrous for you to invest in something that can fall in value with no warning. Using the wrong investment vehicle could mean, for example, that you would not be able to complete the purchase of your home.

For most investors, financial independence in retirement is the most important goal and it is the longest-term of all their goals. With good health, most investors should plan to be in retirement for 20 to 30 years. Some of their retirement capital will be used up in the early years of retirement, but other amounts will not be spent until near the end of their lives, or will be passed on to future generations. If the investor is in her thirties, it may be 50 to 60 years before the last of her capital is used up. Most investors should therefore have a portion of their capital earmarked for the very long term. Even if you are already in retirement, you may still have a life expectancy of another 25 years or more. Common stock, that is, equity investments, should normally be included as part of an investment portfolio designed for very long-term goals.

Because they want to avoid the volatility that comes with owning equities, some investors decide to use short-term investments, such as bonds and T-bills, as the investment vehicle to achieve their long-term goals. The strategy usually doesn't work because the after-tax rate of return on their short-term investments is not high enough to provide for the necessary capital growth.

If an investment is going to be held for 20 or 30 years, the only important value is the one at the time you sell the investment. This is when the proceeds will be needed to maintain the chosen lifestyle. In this situation, the short-term up-and-down swings in value that occurred during the 20 years you held the investment really do not matter. In the long term, an investment portfolio that includes some common stocks will almost always produce a higher average return.

With proper diversification, you will not be much affected by drops in the stock market index. You won't have to panic when the market falls in value because the drop to your portfolio will be minor. The short-term movements do not matter if you stick with the long-term investment strategy.

When I say that investors should not be concerned about short-term fluctuations, I'm assuming they are in a well-balanced and diversified portfolio. A portfolio that is properly designed to return, say, 8%, is unlikely to decline by more than 10%, during a normal downturn. If it falls by 20% or more, this indicates that the portfolio is very aggressive and not well diversified. In these cases, unless they are content with the possibility of a very large loss, investors should get a second opinion about potential risk.

BOTTOM LINE: Make an estimate of a normal life expectancy and from this number subtract your present age. If the answer is 20 years or more, financial security in retirement is a long-term goal. For most long-term goals, investors should use a diversified portfolio that would include different asset classes, such as bonds, common stocks, income trusts, managed futures, and hedge funds. If you are saving for education, a down payment on a home, or a new car, you should be using short-term investments such as a savings account, GICs, or T-bills.

WHAT YOU CAN DO NOW: Clarify your long- and short-term goals and be sure you are using the right investments for each type of goal.

Part 11

Avoiding Common Financial Pitfalls

"It ain't so much what people know that hurts
as what they know that ain't so."

Artemus Ward,
19th-century American humorist

Tip 87

Don't Believe That the Old Rules No Longer Apply

Investors who believe that "this time it's different" always lose money if they hold on until the bubble bursts.

The market can be a wise teacher or a mocking bystander. As Frank J. Williams, author of *If You Must Speculate, Learn the Rules*, puts it, "If you are intelligent the market will teach you caution and fortitude, sharpen your wits, and reduce your pride. If you are foolish and refuse to learn a lesson, it will ridicule you, laugh you to scorn, break you, and toss you on the rubbish-heap."

When the NASDAQ index was close to its peak, some experts predicted that it would continue to go higher because "this time it was different."

What did "this time" bring us? A new technology in the form of the Internet and computers, more informed investors, baby boomers, and Alan Greenspan and his enlightened interest rate policies. It brought us a strong dollar, more liquidity, low inflation, and an equity "risk premium" that no longer seemed relevant. A greater percentage of investment decisions were made by professionals such as managers of mutual funds, pension funds, and hedge funds. Interest rates and inflation were lower. All of these things combined to create a different environment.

What was the result? Unrealistic expectations resulted in stocks becoming overvalued until the bubble burst and they began to trade based on their real value. After the crash that started in March 2000, stocks traded based on their future potential earnings, not on the belief that the stock could be sold at a higher price to a bigger fool.

When people say that higher prices are justified, they are really saying that common sense rules no longer apply. The common sense rule is that the value of the stock is ultimately tied to the future stream of earnings that the stock is expected to produce. When these rules seem not to apply, the industry will invent new theories to help keep the momentum going. Then the pendulum eventually begins to swing in the other direction and good old common sense returns.

Every speculative bubble period has been driven by this same type of irrational enthusiasm. By some calculations, there have been 18 investment bubbles during the last 200 years. They all ended in the same way.

In the summer of 1720, Sir Isaac Newton said that he could understand the movement of the heavens but not the madness of people who invested in the South Sea Company. Finally, he, too, was caught up in the mania. He invested £20,000 in September, at the very peak of the market, only to see the investment become worthless when the market crashed one month later.

Sooner or later, someone will point out that the emperor has no clothes. As implausible theories are exposed, logic will reign again. The bubble bursts and the unreasonable optimism is replaced by an equal outpouring of pessimism. Yet, the essence of wealth creation never changes: that wealth is accumulated by those who are patient, not impulsive. Those on their way to wealth use common sense, resist the impulse to follow the herd, and diversify to handle all risk.

John Mauldin's book *Bull's Eye Investing* reports on Jeremy Grantham's extensive market trend analysis. Grantham found that in every case of 28 stock market bubbles, the market, after an extraordinary rise in value, always fell back to a level below the average trend line.

BOTTOM LINE: When you see illogical or irrational behaviour in the stock markets, do not believe that the trend will continue forever. The markets move and bubbles are formed based on illogical thinking and the desire to acquire a fast buck. In the long run, the value of a share of a company is always related to the present value of the future earnings of that company.

WHAT YOU CAN DO NOW: Read the book *Yes, You Can Time the Market!* by Ben Stein and Phil DeMuth.

Tip 88

Beware of Anything Promoted as a New Investment Idea

It is a mistake to think that there are many new, better, and easier ways to get rich quick. When investors look for a fast and easy approach, they almost always lose money.

Are we smarter in managing financial matters than those who have gone before us? We certainly have more technology. Even 25 years ago, most of us were making do without computers. However, as Larry Swedroe, author of *What Wall Street Doesn't Want You to Know*, puts it, "There is nothing new—only the history you haven't read." And history tells us that little is new in the markets. For example, Holland, in the 1600s, had a futures and options market featuring some of "advanced" options techniques now known as *collars* and *straddles*. Athens, in 350 BC, had banks offering mortgages and letters of credit.

Since the time of the Roman Empire, cycles of boom and bust, inflation and deflation, speculative excesses and panics have occurred in regular patterns. David Knox Barker writes in *Jubilee on Wall Street* about a banking panic in AD 33 that sounds much like the banking crisis in the early 1930s in North America:

> The important firm of Seuthes and Son, of Alexandria, was facing difficulties because of the loss of three richly laden ships in a Red Sea storm, followed by a fall in the value of ostrich feathers and ivory.
>
> At about the same time the great house of Malchus and Co. of Tyre, with branches in Antioch and Ephesus, went bankrupt when its Phoenician workmen called a strike. The downfall was speeded when the manager was convicted of embezzlement. These failures affected the Roman banking house Quintus Maximus and Lucius Vibo. A run commenced on their bank and spread to other banking houses that were said to be involved.
>
> Tiberius was a wise ruler and solved the problem with his usual good sense. He suspended temporarily the processes of

debt and distributed 100 million sesterces from the Imperial treasury to the solvent bankers to be loaned to needy debtors without interest for three years. Following this action, the panic in Alexandria, Carthage and Corinth quieted.

All of which proves that over thousands of years, very bright people have come up with many different ways to invest other people's money. With each new generation of investors, the same ideas are repackaged to seem new and innovative, but the result is usually the same.

Real wealth is most likely accumulated in one of three ways: by putting together the investment deal yourself, which effectively means packaging and selling investment expertise; by creating your own business; or by saving your money in safe investments and letting the magic of compounding do its work.

During the past 2000 years, the best investing idea—the one that has always worked, the one that guarantees financial security, and the one that is the least complicated—is to save 10% of your income in safe investments. I predict that this strategy will continue to work best in the next decade if not for the next 2000 years.

BOTTOM LINE: An excellent little book on saving is *The Richest Man in Babylon*, by George W. Clason. The book makes a realistic story out of the simple strategy of saving 10% of all you earn. This book should be required reading in every school. If it were, it would go a long way to helping young people become financially secure.

WHAT YOU CAN DO NOW: Forget about finding a fast, new, easy formula that enables you to achieve financial independence in half the time. Plan to become financially secure the old-fashioned way, by controlling your spending and steadily saving your money in safe investments.

Tip 89

Don't Buy Investments that Sound Too Good to Be True

When investors think that they can get higher returns without taking higher risks, they increase the probability of losing a lot of capital. When comparing investments of similar types, there is no such thing as a higher return without higher risk or volatility.

Frank A. Clark, the American philanthropist, once said, "I'd rather see folks doubt what's true than accept what isn't." Conventional wisdom says that if it sounds too good to be true, it probably is. Let's take a look at why this bit of wisdom is ignored and why people still fall for sales pitches.

An example is buying corporate bonds with high interest rates. Some investors may think that the bond market will allow differences in interest rates without a corresponding difference in risk. They don't understand the size and efficiency of the bond market.

For the average investor, it is impossible to find a bond that pays a higher rate of return unless it also involves higher risk. It may be default risk, liquidity risk, interest rate risk, or event risk, but the risk is there whether you see it or not.

If one investment offers a higher interest rate than other investments that appear to have the same risk and maturity, common sense requires you to ask questions. Why is the company that is issuing the security willing to pay an interest rate that is significantly higher than the going rate? The answer is that the company has to offer the higher rate in order to attract buyers.

Professional traders and institutions that make up the bond market and make most of the bond purchases are knowledgeable about risks. They will decline to purchase a bond with higher risk unless the issuer and/or market forces cause the rate of return to increase to compensate for the higher risk.

If you are offered a great investment that is almost too good to be true, ask yourself why the promoters are not taking up all of the investment themselves? Quite simply, in many cases the greatest profit is in the packaging and selling of the business opportunity. The promoters, the financial advisors, and the lawyers make the money. The investor usually loses money.

A mistake that some investors make is to think they will get rich by providing some start-up capital for a new business venture. Such an investment might offer a once-in-a-lifetime opportunity for success, but the odds are very much against this. Most individuals investing in start-ups will lose the money they invest. If you feel you must make an investment of this nature, make sure it does not represent more than 5% of your investment capital.

Financial advisors might recommend investment products, such as income trusts, without understanding the risks involved. During 2003 and 2004, for example, income trusts were one of the best-performing asset classes. An advisor would be wrong, however, if he or she did not point out the significant difference in safety between a government bond paying 4% or 5% interest and an income trust with a 12% yield. If the stock market took a significant downturn, or if the income trust had to cut its distribution, it would become evident that income trusts share characteristics with stocks and fluctuate in value just as stocks do. It would be clear to investors that they were taking higher risks they did not understand fully in order to earn the higher income.

When dealing with individual investments, the old rule that higher return equals higher risk is almost always true. When dealing with diversified combinations of assets, such as in a portfolio put together with investments that have low correlation with each other, the rule is not always true.

Investors should know that there are some investment products, such as a "fund of hedge funds," that combine very different asset classes into the one investment. When several high-risk/high-return investments are selected based on having low correlation, they are unlikely all to go up or down at the same time. Using Modern Portfolio Theory and wide levels of diversification, a higher return with a lower level of risk can be generated for the portfolio as a whole.

BOTTOM LINE: One of the most important services a competent advisor can offer is to help you understand and manage risk. But it is unlikely that even your advisor is smart enough to purchase a bond with a higher yield without some commensurate and offsetting higher risk.

WHAT YOU CAN DO NOW: If you have investments that seem to be paying a higher than normal return, ask your financial advisor to explain what additional risk you are taking. Find out if it is risk related to default, liquidity, events, managers, currency, interest rates, inflation, or something else.

Think Twice about Getting Advice from Friends and Relatives

Unless your friends and relatives are experienced and successful in investing, they are likely operating under the same myths and misconceptions that have been keeping you from being financially secure.

We are all looking for the correct answers to our investment questions. It is natural for us to turn first to the people we trust the most: our friends and relatives. However, two major factors influence the usefulness of investment advice.

First, the person giving the advice should have no motivation other than the desire to help you achieve financial security. In most cases, advice from family and friends scores well on this measure. Most advice from your financial advisor is also in your best interest. There are occasions, however, where the objectivity of this advice is compromised because one choice results in significantly higher one-time commissions or ongoing fees for the advisor than another choice.

The second factor is the quality of the advice, and this is where those close to us do not score so well. Sometimes a well-informed family member—who manages investments personally and studies the market—can be a valuable resource for advice. Make sure, however, that this trusted relative has kept up to date, understands investment theory, knows how to minimize risk, and understands the new investment products. Most of us do not have such a knowledgeable relative, and we are better off to ignore the advice of those close to us.

A good financial advisor will also take into consideration your unique situation. Investments that may be ideal for family or friends may be inappropriate for you and she will tell you so.

You should expect that your financial advisor's advice is based on greater knowledge and experience in investments. If you had a serious medical problem you would go to a doctor, not a relative. The same logic should apply when you need investment advice.

One of the most common mistakes friends and family make when talking about investments is to compare rates of return without comparing risk. It is easy to compare returns but much more difficult to compare risk. Sometimes the friend or relative who boasts of the high return is taking greater risks than even he or she imagines or desires. You can safely assume that any investor who compares rates of return without comparing risk has less investment knowledge than you do.

BOTTOM LINE: Well-intentioned friends and relatives usually have their own biases and subscribe to the same myths and misconceptions as the rest of the public. Weigh their advice carefully and give your financial advisor an opportunity to comment on the recommendations they offer.

WHAT YOU CAN DO NOW: Refuse the advice of friends and relatives unless you are absolutely convinced by the evidence of their investing success that they really are students of the market. Always remember that a proper analysis of investment results requires a comparison of risk as well as return.

Tip 91

Don't Worry about Looking Uninformed

Investors sometimes leave meetings with their financial advisor without really understanding what has been agreed to and what risks are involved.

You need information about what you own in your portfolio, how the investments are being managed, your investment strategy, the level of risk, the expected return, fees, the rate of return you need to earn to achieve your goals, and the actual return you are earning.

Most investors don't have all this information because they weren't told. If the facts were explained at all, they were expressed in a jargon comprehensible only to those in the investment industry. Don't be shy about asking questions. Unless you have taken courses in the subject, investments may be a mysterious world. You have to seek out the answers by asking questions. Be aware, also, that there are no dumb questions, only dumb answers.

Here are some questions you should not be afraid to ask:

- With 95% probability, what is the long-term average rate of return I should expect from this portfolio?
- With 95% probability, what is the best and worst return I should expect in any one-year, three-year, or five-year period?
- What are the risks in this portfolio?
- What could go wrong that would make this portfolio perform worse than expected?
- What one-time and ongoing fees are involved?
- Are there any other fees that are hidden or buried?
- What assumptions are the projected returns based on?
- What is the benchmark against which we can compare results?
- What is the expected Sharpe Ratio of this portfolio?

NOTE: A 95% probability level means that, in 95 years out of 100, the actual return of the portfolio would be expected to fall within the stated range. That means that in 5 years out of 100, the return would be expected to be outside the normal range. You don't mind if it is outside and higher. Statistically, however, it is probable that in the years that the performance is outside the expected range, the actual return will be on the low side rather than the high.

BOTTOM LINE: Unless you have an essential understanding of the facts, your financial security is at risk. Most financial advisors want you to be informed. You should never feel embarrassed to ask whatever questions you need to, in order to get a complete understanding of your portfolio.

WHAT YOU CAN DO NOW: At your next meeting with your financial advisor, ask for a report that shows the expected average return and the expected range of returns for the portfolio as a whole.

Tip 92

Don't Assume You Can Delay Making an Investment Decision

Unless you are in a well-diversified portfolio, the market can be dangerous and unforgiving. If you think you can stop the market forces because you want to make your decision at a more convenient time, you are increasing your odds of losing money.

Investors sometimes feel uncertain about which way to proceed and think they can postpone making a decision. With investing, however, it is impossible to delay a decision: a decision to delay is in fact a decision to stick with the status quo. Doing nothing may be the right decision if you are out of the market and the market is going down, but it may be the wrong decision if you are in the market and a severe market decline is on the horizon.

For example, a few years ago when Nortel was trading at $120, some investors ignored their financial advisors' advice to sell because they wanted to wait until more facts became available. That "do nothing" decision cost them dearly as Nortel fell to under $4 per share. These investors intended to make a decision but were not quite ready. Deciding to do nothing was in effect a decision to hold on to a vastly overvalued stock.

The three possible investment decisions are to buy, sell, or hold. Holding is less obviously a decision but it is a decision nevertheless—a decision not to change the asset mix. If you are in the right asset mix, this may be a wise decision. But if your asset mix should be changed, then doing nothing may be a big mistake.

Investors usually put their capital in three asset classes: stocks, bonds, and cash. Cash, as an asset class, occasionally turns out to be the best performing. An investor who has cash in the bank has decided to invest in cash as opposed to stocks, bonds, real estate, or any other asset class. If the other asset classes fall in value, the decision to stay in cash will have been the best. On the other hand, if the investment that was being considered rises in value, and now more cash is required to purchase the same investments, then this was not the best decision. The decision to do nothing can have just as big an impact on your financial future as the decision to buy or sell. Do not be misled into thinking that you can avoid making investment decisions. You can delay the decision to buy and you can delay the decision to sell, but this only means that you are making the decision to hold.

BOTTOM LINE: Doing nothing is an investment decision. It is a decision not to change your asset allocation. It may be the right decision or it may be the wrong decision, but investors should not deceive themselves into thinking that they can avoid or delay making investment decisions.

WHAT YOU CAN DO NOW: Take a look at the way you make investment decisions. Ask yourself if you have done all you can to get a financial plan, to understand your investment strategy, and to take control of your finances. Spend a few moments imagining how the decision to do nothing, to leave things as they are, may hurt your retirement plans.

Tip 93

Don't Hold on to an Investment That Is not Good Enough to Buy

Holding on to a bad investment and hoping that it will increase in value to some arbitrary level is usually a "loss denial" reaction. Hanging on is an emotional rather than a logical response. The longer it takes to recognize a mistake, the longer it will take to begin correcting the problem.

Investors sometimes become emotionally attached to securities and hang on to them when logic and common sense dictate that they should be sold. Holding on to a losing investment because it may recover its value helps them avoid acknowledging the truth about their loss.

If an investor is very unhappy with the performance of a stock, it is unlikely that she will buy more at the current price. The idea of buying more simply makes no sense if better investment opportunities are available. Yet, even with better opportunities available, investors will often refuse to sell an underperforming stock. This makes no sense. Why would they tie up capital in positions that they wouldn't invest in now with better opportunities being readily available?

A simple rule applies: if you don't have enough confidence to buy, at today's price, more of an investment you own, you should sell it and put your money to work in better investment opportunities. More good investments are available than you could possibly include in your portfolio. The dilemma is how to choose among such excellent candidates. This being the case, there is no way you should hang on to an investment that is so bad that you wouldn't want to buy it again. The market is saying what this investment is really worth and all the hope in the world will not bring about a revaluation. The investment's value has just as much chance of falling further as it has of rising.

Here are some examples of situations where there's no valid reason to continue to hold an investment:

- The investment (or the individual company) no longer offers the same prospects and promise that it did at the time of purchase.
- The investment no longer fits in the portfolio because the risk and return objectives of the portfolio have changed.

- The investment should be trimmed back to rebalance the portfolio to the desired asset mix.
- The existing investment has the same potential as when you bought it, but better, more flexible, and safer investment choices have become available.

When any of these conditions exists, the investment should be sold at once. An exception is the case where there is an accrued capital gain. It might make sense to delay for a month to push the gain into the next taxation year. If you are not satisfied with the investment, however, the more likely scenario is that by selling the investment you will trigger a capital loss.

BOTTOM LINE: You should not continue to hold any investment that you do not believe represents good value at today's market price. If it represents good value at today's price you should be willing to buy more of it, subject to the rule that you never want to have more than 10% of your portfolio invested in any one security.

WHAT YOU CAN DO NOW: If you own a security that you would not buy at today's market price because you think there are better opportunities for investing your money, sell the security and put the proceeds to work where you expect a better chance of increasing your return.

Don't Think That the True Value of a GIC Does not Fluctuate

When investors buy bank-issued guaranteed investment certificates (GICs) rather than corporate bonds issued by the same bank, they lose something in the rate of return and they give up liquidity.

As a general rule, I do not recommend buying guaranteed investment certificates (GICs).

Many investors who buy GICs do so for the wrong reasons, chiefly for the insurance protection of the Canada Deposit Insurance Corporation (CDIC) and the belief that a GIC does not fluctuate in value.

Experienced investors rarely buy GICs. They know they can almost always get a higher return with no additional risk, and also have daily liquidity, by buying the corporate bonds issued by the same entity that is issuing the GIC. For example, a portfolio of Royal Bank GICs usually will pay less than Royal Bank corporate bonds with the same maturity dates.

It is unlikely that the Royal Bank of Canada will ever default on either their outstanding GICs or their bonds. In the unlikely event that one of the major Canadian banks fails, it could mean that they all fail. In this highly unlikely scenario, there would not be enough money for the CDIC to bail out all investors. Therefore, for investors dealing with one of the major Canadian banks, the CDIC insurance is probably unnecessary during good times, and might not be enough protection in the event of a collapse of the entire banking system.

One thing that makes GICs so attractive to inexperienced investors is the illusion that the certificates do not change in value. They have this idea because the GIC is always shown at the same value each month on their account statements. The reason for this is that the issuer does not report the real value on a monthly basis. Instead, the issuer shows the investor only the value at maturity. That is logical. If the investor is unable to cash in a GIC before the maturity date, the current market value is of little importance.

This differs from reporting the value of bonds. The true market value of the bond is reported each month. This value will change in response to changes in interest rates. If interest rates rise, the market value of the bond will fall, and if interest rates fall, the market value will rise. In the reporting of bond value, you are given the true current market value and, in the case of the GIC, you are being shown the maturity value rather than the true current market value.

BOTTOM LINE: The true market value of a GIC changes as interest rates change in the economy. Since you can't cash the GIC in before the maturity date, the maturity value, not the market value, is shown in monthly reports. If the market value were shown, you would see that it changes in the same way that a bond with the same maturity date changes.

WHAT YOU CAN DO NOW: If you are thinking about buying a GIC (and for most investors there are better choices), obtain a quote for the rate you can get from a corporate bond issued by the same bank that issues GICs. Make certain that the corporate bond is for the same term to maturity as the GIC. Make your decision based on the rate of return, as well as on the value you place on the liquidity and on the security of CDIC coverage.

Never Assume There Is No Loss If You Hold Bonds to Maturity

Not recognizing a loss when it occurs makes it more likely that you will repeat the mistake.

If you own long-term bonds and interest rates rise, your bonds will fall in value. This is because the relatively lower rate of interest being paid on your bond makes the bond less attractive in an environment where higher interest rates are available.

Some investors see this as a "paper loss" because they intend to hold their bonds until maturity. It is easy to see why investors fall into this trap.

The loss is calculated as follows: assume you purchase a $100,000 Government of Canada 10-year bond with a coupon interest rate of 6%. Soon after you pay $100,000 for the bond, interest rates increase sharply and the market value of this bond drops to $80,000. Your financial advisor tells you that you don't really have a loss if you hold the bond to maturity, at which time you will receive the face value of $100,000. Also, every year during the next 10 years, you will get the $6,000 of interest you expected to receive. So where is the loss, unless you decide to sell?

In the real world, the loss exists. At the current reduced price, someone else with only $80,000 can now buy the identical bond that has the face value of $100,000. The new buyer will collect the same amount at maturity and the same annual interest payments. So, if someone else can buy, for $80,000, the same security that you purchased for $100,000, the market is telling you plainly that you have lost $20,000 at that point. The market is also telling you that the return you earn, from that time forward until the maturity date, is going to be made up of the coupon interest plus $2,000 per year of capital appreciation (because the bond is going to grow in value from $80,000 to $100,000 over the next 10 years).

In some instances, when a loss occurs, the prudent move may be to sell. In other instances, it may be wise to invest more heavily in the asset that has fallen in value. Regardless, you should recognize that you have had a real loss, even if it is a "paper loss" not applicable for income tax purposes.

BOTTOM LINE: A paper loss is a real loss. Just because you have a loss does not, however, always mean you should sell the investment. Perhaps you should buy more at the lower price.

WHAT YOU CAN DO NOW: Remove the words "paper loss" from your vocabulary. Be suspicious if your financial advisor tells you not to worry because "it is only a paper loss."

Tip 96

Don't Confuse the Bond Yield with the Bond Coupon

In a non-RRSP portfolio, if bonds have to be sold, it usually makes more sense, from the after-tax point of view, to sell the bond with the highest coupon rate rather than the one with the lowest. When investors confuse the real yield and the coupon yield, they often decide to sell the wrong bond.

Some investors think that a particular interest-bearing investment is paying a higher rate of return than it really does, and they are therefore reluctant to sell it.

Here is how the problem arises. Assume a government or corporate bond—not a Canada Savings Bond—was issued when interest rates were higher than they are today. The coupon rate on this bond is, say, 8%, the prevailing rate when the bond was issued. Investors who own the bond receive an interest payment every year equal to 8% of the face value of the bond. If the face value of the bond was $100,000, that means that $8,000 of interest payments will be received each year.

Investors are pleased with this rate of return, particularly if the current interest rate falls below 4%. They think they are earning twice as much as a comparable bond on the market today.

What they are overlooking, however, is the efficiency of the bond market. As interest rates change, the market value of bonds also changes. An investor who wants the security of a government bond will pay a premium for one that pays 8% when the new government bonds are only paying 4%. For a bond that matures in one year, the amount of the premium would be about $4,000.

If you paid $104,000 for a bond that would earn $8,000 interest and return $100,000 in one year, your real return would be $4,000. Equally, if you pay $100,000 for a bond that would earn $4,000 and would return your capital of $100,000 in one year, you also earn $4,000. In both cases, the return is about 4%. In the first instance, $8,000 of interest is earned but there is a $4,000 loss on the capital, because the bond pays only $100,000 at maturity. In the second case, there is simply $4,000 of interest earned. Therefore, the real return for the bondholder who holds on to the bond is the taxable interest coupon received—$8,000 less the $4,000 decrease in market value that occurs over the remainder of the year ($104,000 –$100,000 = $4,000). So, the real return is about the same as a bond that has a 4% coupon.

One potential disadvantage of holding the bond to maturity is that the holder will receive T5 slips for the actual $8,000 of coupon interest received. There is, in theory, an offsetting deduction for the capital loss on the bond. However, in practice, the capital loss can only be offset against a capital gain. Even at that, the loss is only one-half deductible.

If the bond has several years before it matures, there is a greater advantage to having a higher coupon rate, and the market price of the bond will be much higher. However, because of the way the market works to increase or decrease the asking price, the true yield will generally be the same for all bonds with similar quality and similar term to maturity. There are many reasons why you might decide to sell or to keep a certain investment, but your decision is more likely to be the wrong one if you do not understand the difference between the real yield and the coupon yield.

BOTTOM LINE: It is the yield to maturity, not the coupon yield, that tells you the true rate of return you will earn for a particular bond. Sometimes, and mainly for income tax reasons, it might make sense to sell a bond with a high coupon and reinvest in a bond with a lower coupon but similar yield to maturity.

WHAT YOU CAN DO NOW: If you are going to sell bonds, consider both the coupon rate and the yield to maturity before you decide which one to sell.

Tip 97

Don't Believe It's a Loss Only If You Sell It

When investors don't recognize that a loss is a loss, they may be underestimating the risk of their portfolio as a whole, and they may be postponing important adjustments to their portfolio and lifestyle.

As already discussed, a loss is a loss. A paper loss is a loss that has not been realized by selling the investment. Novice investors are sometimes prone to denying reality by not recognizing a loss. Also, financial advisors, when facing angry clients, might be tempted to encourage the belief that paper losses are nothing to be concerned about. It may not be a loss for income tax purposes until you sell it, but it is definitely a loss in terms of calculating your net worth.

Living under this illusion can be a problem because it may cause you to delay making important decisions. Often, the right thing to do is to take corrective action as soon as things start to go wrong. A saying in the industry suggests that your first loss is often your best loss.

Like all myths, this one has some grounding in reality. The value of an investment fluctuates every day and a small loss may indeed be recovered the following day. That the investment may rebound tomorrow does not, however, indicate that a real loss has not occurred today.

When you call a loss a loss, you recognize your mistake. Being aware of a mistake is more likely to lead you to corrective action. Unfortunately, investors, like most people, don't want to recognize mistakes and often will grasp at any straw to avoid facing reality. I know of one investor who had almost 50% of his assets invested in Cisco Systems when it was trading at $65 per share. When Cisco dropped to $15 per share, common sense suggested that he should reduce his retirement spending plans. Yet he clung to the belief that it was only a paper loss and, since paper losses don't matter, he continued with a higher level of spending than was sustainable in view of his reduced circumstances. By clinging to this false hope, he further damaged his future financial security.

The stock market shows you the true value of your investments. When value increases, they are bid higher. When value decreases, they are marked down. This is the way the industry reports gains and losses. It should also be the way you recognize a loss when it has occurred.

BOTTOM LINE: If something had a higher value when you purchased it than it does today, you have lost money.

WHAT YOU CAN DO NOW: Forget the idea that a paper loss is less serious than a realized loss. Start measuring your net worth based on the true value of what you have today, not on some fantasy that distinguishes between paper losses and real losses.

Tip 98

Never Become Mesmerized by the Most Obvious Risk

You can't predict what the major risks will be over the next 20 years. The sensible thing to do, therefore, is to be fully diversified to protect yourself against many risks.

Everyone knows that money can be lost as the result of buying risky stocks. In the short term, you can lose money even when you purchase what are considered to be safe blue-chip stocks. Some people believe that it is not safe to be in the market at all. Retired people are particularly vulnerable to this fear. As a result, they often focus too much on stock market risk, while overlooking other risks, such as inflation. The most important risk, however, is the possibility that you will not have enough money to achieve your financial goals.

You should address all risks that can prevent you from accumulating enough money to retire. Obviously, if you don't save enough, you will not have enough. It is also true that if your savings do not earn enough, you will not have enough. Or if you pay too much in income tax. Or if inflation robs you of your purchasing power. Or if you make money from your stocks but lose because your currency has been devalued.

Here are some more risks. If you invest in stocks you can lose money when the stock market goes down. Your stocks could go down even though the market as a whole goes up. Investing in bonds could result in a loss when interest rates go higher. Your real estate investments could drop in value when interest rates go up, or if there is deflation. If you invest in T-bills, you can lose an opportunity when interest rates go lower.

If all your capital is invested in foreign-currency-denominated investments, and the Canadian dollar appreciates in value, you are going to lose some of your capital. The point is, it is difficult for most investors to achieve their financial goals solely by avoiding stock market risk. Investors who take no more risk than absolutely necessary will still benefit from having some exposure to the stock market.

The best way to address all risks is to be well diversified. The old adage of not putting all your eggs in one basket is still the best advice for reducing risk. A sensibly diversified portfolio should include cash, short-term bonds, long-term bonds, income trusts, common stocks (most likely held through a mutual fund or an ETF), managed futures, and a fund of hedge funds (preferably one where the capital is guaranteed). The percentage of your portfolio allocated to each category will vary. If some of your capital is invested in each of these categories, you will have protection against a greater number of risks than if you have all your capital invested in very "safe" things like government bonds.

BOTTOM LINE: Don't focus all of your investment strategy on avoiding a single risk. The biggest risk is not having enough money in your retirement. The way to minimize that risk is to be properly diversified.

WHAT YOU CAN DO NOW: Review your asset mix to be certain that you are adequately diversified.

Tip 99

Don't Focus on the Wrong Investment Issues

When investors focus on the wrong issues, over which they have no control, they lose focus over what they can control: their spending and the monitoring of their portfolio.

The eminent French writer Jules Renard once said, "I finally know what distinguishes man from beasts: financial worries." Investors tend to worry about short-term fluctuations in the stock and bond markets, currency, interest rates, and income tax. These issues have some importance, but they are beyond investors' control.

Here is what investors should worry about:

- Not knowing the rate of return needed in order to achieve financial goals
- Not knowing how to control spending so that 10% of income can be saved consistently
- If you are already retired, not knowing how much can be safely spent without running out of money
- Not knowing if the asset mix is sensible and can earn the rate of return needed to achieve financial goals
- Not asking the right questions
- Not having a properly diversified portfolio

The answers to these issues can all be found when you have a properly prepared financial plan and an investment strategy designed to earn the required rate of return with the least amount of risk possible.

BOTTOM LINE: If you are saving 10% of your income and your portfolio is properly diversified, you are going to become financially independent regardless of stock market fluctuations, interest rate changes, income tax, and currency changes.

WHAT YOU CAN DO NOW: Find out if you are in the asset mix that can be expected to earn the rate of return you need.

Part 12

Following the Path to Financial Happiness

"The human species, according to the best theory
I can form of it, is composed of two distinct races:
the men who borrow and the men who lend."

Charles Lamb,
English essayist and poet

Tip 100
Understand the Secret of Financial Security

Security and happiness are the ultimate goals! Having an ever-increasing level of income is not the secret of financial security. Rather, it is learning to live with what we have. We can always aim for a higher income, but until we actually earn that income, we should understand how to be happy with what we have today.

Our ability to imagine new things that we would like to own will always exceed our ability to generate the income necessary to pay for them. No amount of income or capital will ever be enough to fulfill all of the desires that we can imagine. Human nature is such that we always want something more. J. Paul Getty once said, "Money doesn't necessarily have any connection with happiness; maybe with unhappiness." As a prominent oil tycoon with a tumultuous private life, he knew what he was talking about.

We can always think of more ways to spend money than to earn it. Our imagination can take us many places, such as to a larger home in a better area. We can price new and better vehicles, and dream about longer and more exotic vacations. If we plan to postpone happiness until we get all the things we want, we will never be happy.

Some of the best financial planning advice of all time is found in Henry David Thoreau's book *Walden*. Thoreau compares the happiness he enjoyed while living the simple life with that of his neighbour who was caught on the treadmill of having to earn an ever higher income to support his lifestyle. His neighbour worked constantly and most of his earnings went toward costs related to his work. He had to rent a house close to where he worked, and he needed to buy heavy work clothes, work boots, and equipment. His work was so hard he had to eat a richer diet that included more protein; and he had to buy meat because he had no time to fish.

Meanwhile, Thoreau did not have to travel to work every day. He had time to catch fish for food. With his free time, he built his own home so he didn't need money to pay rent. Since his needs were limited, he only had to work occasionally to earn money for basics like salt and sugar. He spent his time doing what he wanted to do, which was to read and write.

A parallel can be drawn from today's frenetic world of work. For instance, many young married couples both need to work to have what their working lifestyles demand. They need two cars, costly daycare, an expensive house near work, fashionable work clothes, and more meals out, because both are too tired to cook. After paying for all that, much of the additional money they earn goes to income tax.

Most people are happier when they take control of their health, lose weight, and begin an exercise program. In the same way, most people are happier when they take control of their finances and begin to live within their means.

Ultimately, we are all forced to live within our means. Some of us will incur debt to get material things sooner rather than later. The day of reckoning is delayed, but there comes a time when we can't borrow any more. That's the point when all of us have to live within our means. For those who take responsibility, and define their limits for themselves—for example, being willing to spend only 90% of what they earn while saving the rest—it is only a matter of time before they will become wealthy.

BOTTOM LINE: Unless your spending is under control, a higher income will not lead to more happiness. However, learning to live within the income that you do have can give you happiness, financial security, and wealth.

WHAT YOU CAN DO NOW: Read the books *Your Money or Your Life* by Joe Dominguez and Vicki Robin and *Getting a Life* by Jacqueline Blix and David Heitmiller.

Tip 101

Don't Incur Too Much Debt by Spending Beyond Your Means

Being in debt is costly. When you pay interest, what you buy can end up costing two or three times the purchase price. If your savings program is delayed by debt, your retirement date may also be delayed for many years.

"You want 21 percent risk free? Pay off your credit cards." So says Andrew Tobias, US political activist and co-creator of a software program called Managing Your Money. The current high level of personal debt is a major problem for both individuals and for society. It is more serious now than a few years ago. Why? While interest rates are low today, this level of debt will be much harder to service when interest rates eventually increase.

Understanding the huge benefit of not spending more than you earn provides an incentive to begin living within your means. Another incentive comes from knowing how much the cost of a purchase is increased when the payment is spread over many years. For example, let's look at the payments that might face a student who has $10,000 in credit card debt at graduation.

For the next 20 years, assume charges are incurred and minimum payments are made, but the balance on the credit card stays at $10,000. Over these two decades, the cost of delaying the payment of the principal could amount to about $40,000. This is the amount of interest that the student may have to pay during that period.

A different result would have been achieved if the student had not made additional purchases on his credit account until the $10,000 was fully repaid. In this scenario, the only difference is that purchases were delayed until the original $10,000 was paid off. Imagine that the amount that would have been spent on interest was invested instead in a diversified investment portfolio. That investment might now be worth about $80,000 to $100,000.

In a debt-free situation, you do not have to eliminate personal spending; you simply have to delay it until you have the cash. In the debt-free mode, not only can you spend more but you also will enjoy life more because you will not be feeling as much stress due to debt.

We can get more pleasure from taking the steps that will put us on the path to financial security than we can get from spending more money. Instead of enjoying the new TV, vehicle, or wardrobe, we can enjoy continuing to use our current possessions while we imagine how great it will be when we have financial security and can spend what we want without incurring any debt. Instead of feeling guilty, we can begin basking in the knowledge that we are doing the right thing and that we are going to be financially independent some day soon.

Very few investments can be guaranteed to earn 19% per year, which is the interest rate often charged on credit cards. A credit card balance of $10,000, with an interest rate of 19%, adds up to interest payments of $1,900 per year. Depending on your income tax rate, you would have to earn almost 30% more in order to have 19% left over after tax. By staying out of debt and investing the money that otherwise would be paid in interest, the average person beginning to save today will be wealthy by the time retirement arrives.

Why do we find it so difficult to save? Spenders think that they don't earn enough to save. One problem is that they don't know what their savings target should be in order to provide a good lifestyle in retirement. In most instances, people have enough income to make it worthwhile to begin saving now.

For many, just getting started in a savings program is the most difficult part. Many put off doing this because they think they have no surplus income to save. They plan to start saving when their income increases. This approach almost never works because spending always increases at a faster rate than income.

Unless you have thought seriously about saving, you may not think it important to save more when you receive a small salary increase. The priorities may be purchasing a new wardrobe, eating out more often, or acquiring some new toys and better furniture. And when your income goes significantly higher, your first desire may be a new house, a new car, and expensive vacations. Within a few months, your fixed expenses are once again so high that you think that there is no room to save.

BOTTOM LINE: The solution is to recognize that the problem is spending too much—which means spending beyond your means—not earning too little.

WHAT YOU CAN DO NOW: Make a commitment to enjoy financial security and to achieve your financial goals. Start to save at least 10% of your gross income. Don't let your basic cost of living increase until you are certain that, even with the increase, you can still save that 10%.

Tip 102

Know When to Cut Back on Fixed Monthly Payments

Because we do not focus on the consequences of debt, we are more likely to fall prey to the advertising of companies that make profits through our debt. If we can see the problems that debt brings, we will find it easier to resist the pressure to take on more debt each month.

Fifty years ago, before credit was so easily available, people wanting to purchase an automobile or go on a vacation saved their money each month. When they had enough money saved up, they made the purchase. After buying the item, their monthly cash flow actually increased because they no longer had the need to set aside the monthly amount.

Today, we hardly have enough time to decide if we really want the item before it is on the VISA card. A long-weekend vacation, for example, is over and forgotten before the charge for it appears on our statement. We may be paying for that spree for many years.

The obligation to pay fixed monthly expenses does not disappear if we lose our jobs or our circumstances change for the worse in some other way. We're still faced with payments for the car, the loan, the mortgage, and the credit cards. On the other hand, if our overspending is done without incurring debt, then in a pinch we can stop travelling, cut back on entertainment, stop buying new clothes, and stop going out on the town. We no longer have that option to cut back if our overspending is in the form of fixed payments for loans and mortgages. Like diamonds, these debts are forever.

If you are in the latter situation, your priority should be first to pay off the debt with the highest interest charge. When that debt is retired and you no longer have to make that monthly payment, allow yourself a small celebration. After that, you can get back to paying off the rest at an even faster rate because you now have the cash that was being used to pay off the debt with the higher rate of interest.

With some types of debt, you may not be permitted to increase the monthly payments. In these cases, you should try to build up your savings account until you have enough to pay off the debt in full. You could turn this into a game. Imagine that you are in a *Survivor*-like challenge and the winner is the contestant who pays down the largest percentage of debt within one year.

Debt levels are higher today than they were a generation ago. Because often both spouses are working, the high level of debt is more worrying than it was in one-income families, where expenses were adjusted to one salary, fixed expenses were lower, and consumer debt was less common. If the wage earner became unemployed, the spouse could usually find employment to bring in some additional income to help get over the crisis. Now, with both spouses already working, the probability of at least one family wage earner losing a job is twice as high. With the income from both spouses needed to take care of debt, even a small setback can grow into a financial crisis.

Within a family, whether or not there are two incomes, fixed expenses should not exceed what can be handled by the top wage earner. At this level of fixed expenses, there is room for savings, and also the flexibility to reorganize financial affairs if one person should become unemployed.

BOTTOM LINE: Becoming financially secure does not have to be complicated. You must decide, however, to eliminate your consumer debt. Once your debt is eliminated, each month put the amount that used to be spent in interest payments into a safe investment. Time and the magic of compounding interest will do the rest.

WHAT YOU CAN DO NOW: Read the book *The Two-Income Trap* by Elizabeth Warren and Amelia Warren Tyagi. They explain why many people with college degrees, good jobs, and their own homes are becoming trapped by debt, and they provide a practical solution for getting out of the debt trap.

Tip 103

Get Used to the Idea that Saving Money Can Be Fun

We enjoy almost everything we buy more when we plan for the purchase and when we save and make some sacrifice for it.

Some people take a long-range view. They look forward to the day when they will have more money and the chance to do more than they can afford right now. It requires a certain confidence in the future to put off enjoying the luxuries of life at this moment. Most people, however, don't want to wait. They put off saving because they think it is more fun to spend their money now.

To encourage saving, we have to change our view of the process; we need to see it not as a pleasure-reducing behaviour but as a pleasure-enhancing one. Instead of thinking about saving as denial and as doing without, you can think of it as getting more of what you want. Think of saving as a game where you are sure to win if you follow simple rules.

Here is a real-life example. A friend of mine and his wife had no money but decided that they wanted a cottage. They estimated that they would need about $30,000 to purchase the land. They pursued their dream by using a giant picture of a cottage similar to the one they had in mind. On the picture they placed a paper with grid lines that contained 30 squares. Every time they saved another $1,000, they cut away one of the squares to reveal their dream cottage.

While saving and cutting away squares, they had great fun making plans and talking about how they would enjoy the cottage. They thought hard about the kind of deck they wanted, a process that required looking at six plans before finally settling on one. They talked about the boating that they would do and how the children would grow up thinking of the cottage as their home.

The cottage did get built. Years later, my friends decided that they had even more fun in the planning and saving stage than they did in owning the cottage.

This couple confirmed something that many of us already know: that saving money for retirement, a vacation, or anything else need not be a painful process. When people hurry off, without much thought, to buy a trip on credit, they miss out on the joy of planning and anticipation.

BOTTOM LINE: Watching your savings grow can be a rewarding experience. In almost all things, if you want to maximize your pleasure, you should take it slowly. Enjoy the anticipation, the planning, the learning, and the saving stages as well as the actual event.

WHAT YOU CAN DO NOW: Think of something you want and start a special savings account for this purchase. Each time you put some money into the account, stop and enjoy some time thinking about how much fun you are going to have when you finally have enough saved up to make the purchase.

Establish an Emergency Fund

It is a mistake not to have a financial reserve – eventually, everyone will be hit with some unexpected cash requirement. Without ready access to a cash reserve, additional costs will be incurred or opportunities lost.

Financial problems are exacerbated when money is needed and there is no emergency fund. Without such a fund, you can fall into a deep financial hole.

Financial emergencies come in many forms. They can result from accidents, illness, funeral expenses, job loss, natural disasters, the need to help a family member, unexpected legal fees, or an income tax reassessment. Problems related to marriage or divorce also can bring about an urgent need for money. Faced with such circumstances, you may be forced to cash in an RRSP or to take even more drastic steps. The choices may be to pay a high income tax penalty, borrow at very high interest rates, or sell an asset at a fire-sale price.

People are more likely to make costly financial mistakes when they are under extreme financial pressure. The feelings of fear and panic will surface more quickly when you need cash and you are without an emergency cushion. A financial reserve protects you from making such mistakes.

The size of the emergency fund depends on a variety of individual circumstances, including the availability of credit, the availability of assistance from family if needed, and a person's age and level of job security and health coverage. A self-employed person needs a larger emergency fund than a government employee who has a pension plan and an excellent health care plan. As a general rule, it makes sense to have a reserve fund equal to about four to six months' net take-home pay.

Some advisors recommend that a reserve fund be kept in liquid investments such as a savings account or T-bills. A disadvantage of this strategy is that the assets earmarked for the emergency fund will earn little income. By keeping money liquid, you are giving up the income that otherwise could be earned on these assets. Other advisors recommend overcoming this disadvantage by using a pre-approved line of credit as the emergency fund.

The important point is that you must have access to a source of funds if an emergency arises. It's your choice whether it is cash in a savings account or an unused line of credit.

Payday loan companies lend money to their clients just until their next payday. More than 10% of Americans reportedly use these services at their exorbitant loan rates, which confirms the seriousness of not having a financial reserve. Those who have such a reserve would agree with the poet Lord Byron, who said, "Ready money is Aladdin's lamp."

BOTTOM LINE: Quick access to cash will give you a sense of freedom and security.

WHAT YOU CAN DO NOW: If you do not have a cash reserve, make it a top priority to establish one equal to at least three months' net income. This is so important that it should take priority even over paying down fixed debt.

Tip 105

Take Advantage of Government Grants for Education

It is critical to begin saving for your children's university education early, for two reasons: (1) you need the time to let compounding work and (2) you want to receive as many annual Canada Education Savings Grants (CESGs) from the federal government as possible.

Next to income tax and interest expense, higher education is one of the largest expenses for a family that sends one or more children to university. This cost can become a crippling debt for parents and/or students if the full cost of education has to be borrowed because money has not been put aside.

The cost of a four-year university program can range between $40,000 and $100,000 per student. If this cost is planned for, the expense becomes manageable. Most parents are of the opinion that students should assume a portion of the cost. Students may do this through summer jobs or by getting student loans. The conventional thinking suggests that when students pay some of the cost, they will have greater appreciation of the chance to continue their education. Students who make some sacrifice to attend university are more likely to work hard at their studies.

Even if the son or daughter pays one-third of the total cost, the parents may end up paying roughly $40,000 in today's dollars. With an average return of 6%, they can meet this need if they save $30 a week beginning when each child is born. This calculation assumes that each child has a Registered Education Savings Program (RESP), which entitles the plan's beneficiary to receive an annual Canada Education Savings Grant (up to the year he or she turns 18) of 20% of the amount contributed, subject to an annual limit of $400.

Thirty dollars per week per child is not insignificant, particularly if two or more children are planning on university, but if this is an important goal, most families can find a way to do it.

BOTTOM LINE: The costs of university education are manageable for most parents if they start saving the day their child is born. Parents should also take advantage of the tax break and the grant offered through the RESP program.

WHAT YOU CAN DO NOW: Speak to your financial advisor or type in "Registered Education Savings Plans (RESP)" into an Internet search engine for more information.

Tip 106

Don't Confuse Income with Cash Flow

Investors can lose out in several ways when they insist on using income-producing investments to satisfy a monthly cash-flow requirement.

Investors who need a monthly cash flow to live on sometimes change from a diversified portfolio, which holds both income-producing and capital-gains-producing investments, to a portfolio that holds only income-producing investments. They make this mistake because they don't understand how easy it is to convert capital gains to cash flow.

When income is earned, in the form of interest and dividends, it is the same as cash flow. However, when income is earned in the form of capital gains, it has to be realized—that is, it has to be sold—before it becomes part of your cash flow. In other words, you have to take one more step before you can spend the money.

There is also an income tax advantage to getting your cash flow from growth investments. If you sell only part of the investment that has the accrued capital gain, part of the payment you receive will be a return of your capital and another part will be "realized capital gains." This means that part of the cash flow (the return of your capital) is not taxable.

For example, assume you have an after-tax cash-flow requirement of $12,000 per year or $1,000 per month, you have $400,000 of capital, you are in the top tax bracket in Ontario, and you can earn 5.5% on a diversified portfolio of government and corporate bonds. One choice to earn your required cash flow would be to invest your entire portfolio in bonds. If you did this, the after-tax income would be about equal to your cash-flow requirement (an income of $22,000 less taxes of $10,100 for a net income of $11,900).

The other choice would be a diversified portfolio with, say, one-half invested in bonds and one-half invested in different types of growth investments. In this case, the bonds will produce about $6,000 of after-tax cash flow, but the growth investments, which we assume will grow at 10%, produce nothing in the way of cash flow. So, $6,600 of the growth investments will have to be sold to generate the necessary cash flow. Of this $6,600 realized from the growth investments, only about $600 represents a taxable capital gain. The rest is non-taxable because it is a return of your capital. Instead of paying income tax on another $11,000 of interest income, you would have to pay tax on only $600 of capital gains. It makes perfect sense to receive a portion of your income requirements from capital-gain-producing investments.

In this example, you have the $12,000 per year or $1,000 per month you need, you've earned more (capital gains were at 10% compared with interest of 5.5%), and you paid less income tax (about $5,200 instead of $10,100).

Investors may not understand the mechanics of how they receive a monthly cheque when the investment is a capital-gains-producing investment rather than one that pays a monthly income. Getting the actual cash payments into the bank account, however, is a simple process. You simply sell off enough of the portfolio to produce the required cash flow for a six-month period. Put this amount into a money market fund and draw the amount out in monthly payments. When this money is gone, sell off another part of the investment and put this amount into the money market fund and draw it out over the next six months.

Income-producing investments should be part of a diversified portfolio because they will reduce the risk of the portfolio as a whole. It makes sense to purchase these investments to build the diversified portfolio, and it makes no sense to abandon the diversified portfolio and concentrate on income-producing investments just to create the cash for monthly payments.

Investors make an unnecessary distinction between the part of the return that comes from income and the part that comes from capital gains. Remember, capital gains can be converted to cash in the bank easily. What's important is the total income, and the greater the portion of the total earned by capital gains, the better. Generally, 100% of interest income is taxed compared with only 50% of capital gains.

BOTTOM LINE: Don't confuse income with cash flow. If you need money every month to meet your spending needs, your need is for cash flow. The most tax-efficient way to get it is not by earning interest income but by realizing capital gains.

Tip 107
Consider the Annuity Income Tax Angle

Investors should consider annuities. They can offer income tax savings, diversification, and an attractive alternative to fixed-income investments such as bonds or GICs.

A life annuity is a contract with an insurance company. The insurance company contracts to make regular payments to the annuitant (the person who buys the annuity), either for life or a fixed term. The main advantage of an annuity is that the buyer can be confident of a fixed level of income for the term of the annuity.

In cases where the money to purchase the annuity comes from non-RRSP sources, the level of income will, after tax, be higher than from equally secure long-term government bonds. Where money from an RRSP is used to purchase an annuity, the full amount of the annuity is taxable as it is received.

Annuities are considered to be an extremely safe investment, due in part to the strict regulations that govern insurance companies. These regulations ensure that the insurance company will honour commitments made to an annuity purchaser. A fund to which insurance companies contribute is a further guarantee for purchasers of annuities. In Canada, no life insurance annuitant has ever lost money because of the failure of the insurance company to make the promised annuity payments.

Here's an example to help explain the value of annuities. Assume you are in your sixties and you purchase a life annuity for $100,000. At a time when five-year GICs can be purchased to yield 5%, the insurance company might agree to pay you $10,000 per year for life. This is double the $5,000 available from a GIC. In addition, the $5,000 that you would earn from the GIC is fully taxable while only a portion of the $10,000 annuity is taxable. The full amount of the annuity payments is not taxable because, in reality, part of the payments should be considered to be a return of your capital. With a GIC, you still have your capital. With an annuity, you use your capital to purchase a guaranteed income for the rest of your life. After you purchase the annuity, you will always have an income, but you no longer have access to the principal amount.

While annuities may be advantageous to purchasers, there is no question that annuities are also profitable for the insurance company. The insurers make money because they have the expertise to invest in diversified and long-term investment portfolios. For the same or lower risk, and because of their investing expertise and methods to control risk, the insurance company is likely to earn a higher return than the average investor. In addition, because of the way the Income Tax Act works, part of the higher income that you receive comes about because the insurance company has certain income tax breaks that indirectly benefit you, the annuity holder.

Insurance companies base their annuity payouts on an actuarial assessment of clients. Their statistical research provides information on how long the average individual will live and, therefore, how long the companies will have to make the monthly payments. If you have good genes, and you live longer than the average annuitant, you will outlive the insurance averages. The company will lose in the sense that it will make annuity payments for a longer period than planned. The reverse applies if you die at an earlier age than the actuarial projections.

Annuities would not make as much sense if it were only a matter of getting back your own capital and living longer than the average. The deferral of income tax is key in considering annuities as an alternative for a portion of one's retirement capital.

Some investors reject the idea of an annuity because of the concern that when they purchase an annuity their capital is gone and there is nothing left for the estate. This is a legitimate concern if you want to leave an estate for your children. The problem can be dealt with easily by combining a purchase of life insurance with the purchase of the annuity. In this way, at death, the capital that was used to buy the annuity comes back into the estate on a tax-free basis and can be passed on to one's heirs.

In the past, investors have turned away from annuities because of the lack of inflation protection in the traditional annuity product. In recent years, however, insurance companies have offered annuity products that have an optional inflation-protection feature. Since these annuities pose a greater risk for the insurance company, the annuity payments will be lower than the starting payments for a contract that does not have the inflation-protection clause.

Like all investment products, annuities have advantages and disadvantages but at the very least they should be considered as part of a diversified portfolio. For example, if an investor wishes to have some protection against deflation, annuities provide one of the best means. Insurers can offer many different variations and, frequently, if the amount of the policy is large, they will customize an annuity so that it fits an investor's specific needs.

BOTTOM LINE: You should at least consider the advantages of an annuity for a portion of your capital in retirement.

WHAT YOU CAN DO NOW: If you are retired, get an annuity quote for 10% to 15% of your capital and compare the after-tax benefits of this investment with the after-tax benefits of the type of fixed-income investments that you currently are holding.

Tip 108

Don't Try to Do It All Yourself

Overconfidence is one of the main causes of large losses. This applies both to the individual investor and the professional manager.

Charles Dow, who transformed the world of investing with the introduction of the Dow Jones Index to gauge the activity of the stock market, said: "Pride of opinion has been responsible for the downfall of more men on Wall Street than any other factor." Individuals become do-it-yourselfers for one of several reasons:

- Some want to save on fees. The commission on a trade done online with a discount financial advisor will be lower than the commission charged through a full-service brokerage firm. Remember, however, that commissions are negotiable. If you are holding a security for many years, as you should be in most cases, the commission will not be a significant factor in your long-term rate of return. Also, if your advisor brought an excellent investment opportunity to your attention, or helped you avoid mistakes, you should be happy to pay a reasonable fee for the advice. Being a do-it-yourselfer solely to save on fees may not be the most cost-efficient course.
- Others trade on their own because they cannot find a financial advisor they like or trust. They feel that they have been burned too many times and they despair of finding someone who is competent, compatible, trustworthy, and wise. These problems can be corrected if you follow procedures outlined in Part 2 when you select an investment advisor.
- Some investors are more confident of their own abilities than of those of their advisors. Indeed, some are more competent than their advisors and should be making their own investment decisions.

A happy medium can be found between the extreme of accepting no responsibility for your finances—leaving it entirely in the hands of your financial advisor—and micro-managing your advisor to the extent that you become a do-it-yourselfer.

Even investors with the ability and the interest to do everything them-selves will, in most cases, be better off by using at least some brokerage firm services. By working with a full-service firm, you will have access to research and investment products, including new issues and structured products not available to the individual who has an account with a dis-count brokerage firm.

Even if you use your advisor primarily as a sounding board, her advice should be helpful. Advisors from full-service brokerage firms also may have access to the latest risk-management optimization software, which is generally too costly for individuals. Do-it-yourselfers can get the benefits of this soft-ware through their advisors, using it to build low-risk investment portfolios.

Here is a benchmark to use in establishing whether or not you have the skills to do better on your own: the performance of the median balanced no-load mutual fund. This is a simple investment. Purchasing it requires no experience or expertise. Compare your own results, over a three-year period and on a risk-adjusted basis, with the performance of this fund. If your performance is better, you can consider continuing to do it all yourself. If the balanced mutual fund shows a better performance, on a risk-adjusted basis, stick with the professionals. And if you have no idea how to determine whether or not you have done better on a risk-adjusted basis—well, that is proof that you need the help of professionals.

You should not try to be a do-it-yourself investor in individual stocks if you are not prepared to do original research. This means studying the financial statements of the target company and its competitors. If you are getting your investment ideas from reading the newspaper, or from Internet chat rooms, you are almost sure to do poorly.

BOTTOM LINE: Many investors who consistently lose money do so because they don't see the big picture. They study the trees but they don't see the forest.

WHAT YOU CAN DO NOW: Are you a do-it-yourselfer? If so, ask yourself if your investment portfolio is optimized with optimization software. If the answer is no, or if you don't know the answer, you should learn about how optimization can be used to maximize returns for any given level of risk.

Conclusion

Congratulations! If you have read this far, it shows that you have the desire and commitment to become financially independent. These are the most important ingredients. All that remains is to use common sense, avoid being greedy for quick returns, spend less than you earn, invest in safe and sensible securities, and let compounding returns work their magic.

Remember, you also have to take responsibility for your own financial security: you have to look at your portfolio carefully a few times each year, and ask questions if things are not going as you expected.

Many excellent financial advisors will have different ideas as to how clients can achieve financial security. In fact, it is unlikely that you could find two financial advisors anywhere in the country with exactly the same idea of what would be a perfect investment portfolio for you. But that's life; nothing is easy. Armed with what you've learned from this book, and perhaps with an independent second opinion, you should be just fine.

I wish you happiness, health, and financial security.

Acknowledgments

I would like to thank the following individuals who have helped me immensely in bringing this book to light:

Merlin Homer first gave me the idea to write the book. Lauchlin and Dorothy Chisholm helped organize its general format and gave me many helpful suggestions. Arnold Gosewich assisted at the beginning of the project, opened doors, and gave seasoned advice. Donald G. Bastian gave me sound editorial advice and introduced me to all the right people at HarperCollins. At HarperCollins, senior editor Brad Wilson and managing editor Noelle Zitzer were patient, helpful, and a pleasure to work with.

Robert Sealy gave me many hours of his time, sound guidance, and encouragement at each stage of the process. Graham Byron and Dane Morrison, two of the most competent financial advisors I know, gave helpful and insightful feedback on the contents. Steve Kangas did outstanding work giving some sections greater clarity.

I would like to thank John De Goey for his thorough review of the manuscript. Thanks to Anne Holloway for her keen editorial eye, and to Maulik Shah for his indexing talents.

For Further Reading

UNDERSTANDING RISK

Absolute Returns, Alexander M. Ineichen, John Wiley & Sons, 2003.

At the Crest of the Tidal Wave, Robert R. Prechter, Jr., New Classics Library, 1996.

Extraordinary Popular Delusions and the Madness of Crowds, Charles Mackay, Harmony Books, 1980.

Fear, Greed and the End of the Rainbow, Andrew Sarlos, Key Porter Books, 1997.

Fooled by Randomness, Nassim Nicholas Taleb, Thomson Texere, 2004.

The Great Crash: 1929, John Kenneth Galbraith, Houghton Mifflin, 1988.

Irrational Exuberance, Robert J. Shiller, MIT Press, 2000.

Jubilee on Wall Street, David Knox Barker, Prescott Press, 1987.

Managing Risk in Alternative Investment Strategies, Lars Jaeger, FT Prentice Hall, 2002.

Manias, Panics, and Crashes, Charles P. Kindleberger, John Wiley & Sons, 1996.

Market Volatility, Robert J. Shiller, MIT Press, 1993.

Risk Is a Four Letter Word, George Hartman, Hartman and Company, 1992.

Risk Is Still a Four Letter Word, George Hartman, Stoddart, 2000.

Understanding and Managing Investment Risk and Return, David L. Scott, Probus Publishing, 1990.

INVESTING

Asset Allocation, Roger C. Gibson, McGraw-Hill, 2000.

Bull's Eye Investing, John Mauldin, John Wiley & Sons, 2004.

If You Must Speculate, Learn the Rules, Frank J. Williams, Cosimo, 2005.

The Intelligent Investor (4th Edition), Benjamin Graham, Harper Business, 1973.

Investment Psychology Explained, Martin J. Pring, John Wiley & Sons, 1993.

Managing Investment Portfolios: A Dynamic Process, second edition, edited by John L. Maginn and Donald L. Tuttle, Warren, Gorham & Lamont, 1990.

Martin Pring on Market Momentum, Martin Pring, McGraw-Hill, 1993.

The New Investment Frontier II, Howard J. Atkinson with Donna Green, Insomniac Press, 2003.

The Power of Index Funds, Ted Cadsby, Stoddart, 1999.

The Professional Financial Advisor, John J. De Goey, Insomniac Press, 2003.

The Prudent Investor's Guide to Hedge Funds, James P. Owen, John Wiley & Sons, 2000.

A Random Walk Down Wall Street, Burton G. Malkiel, W.W. Norton, 1990.

The Random Walk Guide to Investing, Burton G. Malkiel, W.W. Norton, 2003.

Stop Buying Mutual Funds, Mark J. Heinzl, John Wiley & Sons, 1999.

The 10 Biggest Investment Mistakes Canadians Make and How to Avoid Them, Ted Cadsby, Stoddart, 2000.

The Warren Buffett Portfolio, Robert G. Hagstrom, John Wiley & Sons, 1999.

What Wall Street Doesn't Want You to Know, Larry Swedroe, St. Martin's Press, 2001.
Yes, You Can Time the Market!, Ben Stein and Phil DeMuth, John Wiley & Sons, 2003.

INCOME TAX

50 Tax-Smart Investing Strategies, Kurt Rosentreter, Stoddart, 2000.
The Tax Freedom Zone, Tim Cestnick, Viking Canada, 2002.
Winning the Tax Game 2003, Tim Cestnick, Viking Canada, 2002.

FINANCIAL PLANNING

Free Parking: A Second Look at Financial Planning, Alan Dickson, Preferred
   Marketing, 2001.
Guide to Investment and Financial Planning, Jonathan Pond, New York Institute of
   Finance, 1991.
High Expectations and False Dreams, Jim C. Otar, Otar & Associates, 2001.
How to Get Out of Debt, Stay Out of Debt and Live Prosperously, Jerrold Mundis,
   Bantam Books, 2003.
Is Your Retirement at Risk?, Ranga Chand and Sylvia Carmichael, Stoddart, 2002.
Money Logic, Moshe A. Milevsky with Michael Posner, Stoddart, 1999.
Money 201, Ellen Roseman, John Wiley & Sons Canada, 2003.
Smart Couples Finish Rich, David Bach, Broadway Books, 2001.

ENJOYING A HEALTHY AND HAPPY FINANCIAL LIFESTYLE

The Automatic Millionaire: A Powerful One-Step Plan to Live and Finish Rich
   (Canadian Edition), David Bach, Doubleday Canada, 2003.
Getting a Life, Jacqueline Blix and David Heitmiller, Penguin Books, 1997.
More Than Enough, Dave Ramsey, Penguin Books, 2002.
The Richest Man in Babylon, George S. Clason, New American Library, 1988.
The Two-Income Trap, Elizabeth Warren and Amelia Warren Tyagi, Basic Books, 2004.
Walden; Or, Life in the Woods, Henry David Thoreau, Dover Publications, 1995
   (originally published by Ticknor and Fields, 1854).
Your Money or Your Life, Joe Dominguez and Vicki Robin, Viking, 1992.

Index

About the Author

Warren MacKenzie has more than 20 years of experience in offering financial and investment advice, benefiting all kinds of clients, from those just beginning to build a portfolio to the very wealthy. Following graduation from Saint Mary's University (BA) and Dalhousie University (BEd), he began his career as a teacher and then moved on to become a chartered accountant (CA). He furthered his financial expertise by acquiring accreditation as a certified financial planner (CFP) and as a certified investment management analyst (CIMA). A teacher at heart, Warren has a personal interest in helping people achieve financial security and, ultimately, financial independence.

Warren has worked in the investment industry since 1987. He now runs Second Opinion Investor Services Inc., a fee-only consulting practice in Toronto, Ontario. He doe not sell or manage investments; his services are designed to help investors who have concerns about their investments and who want an independent, unbiased second opinion on their portfolio. You can get in touch with Warren at the address below:

Warren MacKenzie
Second Opinion Investor Services
4141 Yonge Street, Suite 303
Toronto, Ontario
M2P 2A8

ph: (416) 640-0550
e-mail: wmackenzie@secondopinions.ca

Visit Warren MacKenzie's website: **www.secondopinions.ca**